# Making Connections

Building relationships with people at the edge

## Tim Lovejoy

**Scripture Union**

Scripture Union, 207–209 Queensway, Bletchley, MK2 2EB, England.

© Tim Lovejoy 1999

First published 1999

ISBN 1 85999 289 7

Unless otherwise attributed, scriptures are quoted from the *Good News Bible* published by The Bible Societies/HarperCollins Publishers Ltd, UK, © American Bible Society, 1966, 1971, 1976, 1992.

British Library Cataloguing-in-Publication Data
A catalogue record for this book is available from the British Library.

Cover design by ie Design.

Printed and bound in Great Britain by Creative Print and Design, (Wales) Ebbw Vale.

# CONTENTS

## *Thank you*

To everyone at Bridges, especially G J. It was an immense privilege to be part of the project, and it has inestimably shaped my faith and working practice. Thank you so much.

To my Frontier Youth Trust colleagues, for stimulating theological reflection and thinking on what it means to be at the edge; epecially to M L E, for your initial support for this project.

To Pip and the Level Fivers, for the first opportunities to grapple with faith in a challenging context.

To Charles, Christina and Barbara, for significant help with word processing; and to Jo, for the editing.

Finally, to all the many friends who have shown such interest and given encouragement along the way. Cheers!

This book is dedicated with love to my parents, Beryl and Charles.

# INTRODUCTION

I walked across the courtyard towards the blue door. There could be no turning back now.

At the door I set down my heavy suitcase, took a deep breath, to summon up my courage, and stretched out a hand to knock. There was no immediate response. Then noises began to emanate from an unexpected quarter. An upstairs window slowly opened. I waited for a face to appear so that I could explain who I was. Instead, a large plastic receptacle protruded from the window and, seconds later, what seemed like a flood of water crashed down to the ground beside me. I looked up in a mixture of surprise and annoyance, and just managed to glimpse a head hastily disappearing inside. I soon discovered the culprit's name – Marcus. As far as he was concerned, this was a fitting introduction to the Bridges Project. (I will leave you to judge for yourselves.)

You too are standing on the threshold of a journey, during which you will get to know some people and places very well. Allow me, then, to introduce you to them and, in doing so, to explain how this book and its title 'Making Connections' came into being. The vehicle we will be using as we move along the line of introductions is the story in Luke 7:36–50 (you may want to turn to it now). Like me, Jesus also got wet feet, though the cause of his condition was very different from mine. I remember reading about this incident as I grew up. It described a person I admired. Here was a man who was obviously upsetting the authorities and who had the courage to do what was right, even in difficult circumstances. Jesus was prepared to be different, and that was appealing.

A few months after I first went to work at Bridges, I began to write articles about the project for the local church magazine. I quoted from this story in Luke because what really struck a chord with me at the time were the thoughts of Simon the Pharisee:

> 'If this man really were a prophet, he would know who this woman is who is touching him; he would know what kind of sinful life she lives!'
>
> *(Luke 7:39)*

Jesus' unique perceptive abilities meant that he knew exactly who the woman was; and it was precisely because he knew her that he felt it crucial to allow her to respond to him as she did. While I was still very new at Bridges, I realised that many of the project users had lived colourful lives similar to the woman's and that it was our job to work with them in the way Jesus did.

At this point, let me introduce you to Bridges because this book is full of stories about it. Bridges was based in two ex-police houses and mainly served the Hatfield–Welwyn area. It provided an informal centre where people could enjoy a cup of tea and a meal, and participate in trips and activities. Many of its users received help with problems related to homelessness, unemployment, health, welfare rights, family, school, substance abuse and debt. The project also had emergency accommodation for the single homeless aged mainly 16–21. Bridges aimed to offer assistance and friendship wherever asked, and attempted to help people work through their difficulties. In all things, the focus was on encouraging them to help themselves.

The project had been going about ten years when I joined it. It had begun when a group of volunteers recognised the need for daytime provision for young people who were experiencing problems related to drugs and homelessness. A hostel facility came later. The site of the two houses was in fact Bridges' third home, following on from a double-decker bus and an old mortuary respectively! Julie was the project's second co-ordinator. Under her guidance, the work developed significantly as Bridges tried to respond to the changing needs of its users. They usually came to the project from social services care or as a result of broken family relationships. When they later moved into the community, many still visited for friendship, help or just to keep in touch. As more young families grew up from among ex-residents, Bridges developed a crèche so that parents could have a break from their children while participating in project activities.

To run such an extensive operation, Julie established a team of three full-time workers, two full-time volunteers, a part-time secretary and other local helpers. Here are some impressions from Hannah who eventually became project deputy in that team.

The first time I walked into Bridges I was, frankly, scared. It felt chaotic but was buzzing with a sense of warmth and belonging. It was difficult to see, at first sight, who was on the working team and who wasn't; later I realised that this was by design. I knew that I wanted to be a part of this warmth ... I began to understand young people for whom a 'normal' family life had never existed, who are often emotionally immature and insecure through this lack, coupled with the constant rejection of a community expecting a high standard of coping ability and 'life skills'. Young people who live a life inclusive of anger, violence, crime, attempted suicide ... Young people perhaps beginning to trust for the first time ... I began to understand why we continued to support individuals who have had long-term contact, on different levels, with Bridges, and who now have families of their own ... support in this is vital in assisting these families to retain their family units.

Of all the project users I met, Ruth is the one I most naturally think of when reading about the woman in Luke 7:36–50. Ruth began to visit the project three years into my working life there. She was seventeen, slim, blonde and striking – a combination guaranteed to attract attention. She stayed at Bridges for a short while before moving into local accommodation with another female ex-resident. The landlady was also a daytime project user. A few weeks after they arrived to stay, strong rumours began to circulate that a number of different men were regularly to be seen visiting the house. Ruth was a woman whose looks would have made some men shy or reticent around her and prompted others to try hard to win her affection or to gain favours from her. The way her life had apparently gone, I suspect that there were very few who had grown to respect and care for the real person beneath the surface.

Let us use our imaginations for a moment and ponder what might happen if we transpose the story from Luke into the Bridges context.

Local dignitaries, representatives from the diocese and managers of grant-making trusts are coming to visit the project. Along with Bridges workers, they have gathered together for a formal meeting. However, shortly before this meeting begins, Ruth wanders in, seemingly unaware of what is taking place. She glances around, pausing as she sees Jed.

Jed is a young local minister who has recently begun visiting Bridges. Last week, he and Ruth had a long conversation. Ruth goes to sit by his feet (there are no empty chairs and no one offers her a seat). The meeting begins.

Ruth appears restless. She looks up at Jed and then begins to weep. Her apparent sorrow is very moving to the Bridges workers who know her. They have never seen Ruth show such emotion before. Perhaps meeting a man who likes being with her, who is genuinely interested in her, who completely accepts her despite what she has done, has had a profound impact on her. She sees Jed as someone good; his care and understanding has made her think about what she can do to change her life.

Gently Jed lays his hand on her head to comfort her. Meanwhile, her eyes red and her face wet with her tears, Ruth produces a small bottle of expensive perfume. She opens the bottle and begins to dab its contents all over his hands. Soon the smell of perfume fills the room. Meanwhile, the rest of the group look on. Some think Ruth is crazy. Some are curious as to how she can afford

such an expensive luxury. And some are aware of her
reputation locally and are wondering how Jed would know
a woman like that. The workers are sure that the perfume
is either a gift from a punter or the product of illegal
earnings. Most are becoming rather uncomfortable.

I wonder how I would have reacted as a Bridges worker if this had
actually happened? I am sure that, like Simon the Pharisee, I
would have been considerably embarrassed that a special occasion was being overshadowed by someone making such a
spectacle of herself.

Some local Christians were involved in the Bridges Project
when it was in its early, 'Summer Holiday' phase and using the
double-decker bus. Needing advice and support, they contacted
Frontier Youth Trust. How fitting, then, that after Bridges my next
(and current) role was that of Regional Development Advisor for
FYT, covering an area which includes Welwyn–Hatfield.

Let me introduce you to FYT. It is a Christian network dedicated to advancing the kingdom of God by supporting, resourcing
and training those who work, or who encourage work, with disadvantaged young people. Since the 1960s, FYT has been in
touch with paid and unpaid workers like those working on the
bus, Christians involved in outreach work with young people in
the community.

Being at Bridges meant having to live out my faith in a challenging and unfamiliar context. I learnt how valuable it is to talk
about one's work with others and how necessary it is to rely on
God. These discoveries have helped me as I resource others in my
FYT role. I have come to appreciate how Christian mission to
young people at the edge of society is demanding, and takes time
and patience. (Frontier youth workers are missionaries just as
much as those serving in remote corners of the world.) My role
has also given me opportunities for theological and biblical
reflection, which have been a great privilege and have contributed
significantly to this book.

'I tell you, then, the great love she has shown proves that her
many sins have been forgiven' (Luke 7:47): Jesus' response to the

woman highlights another dimension to this issue of building relationships on the frontiers. As they do so, Christian youth workers are endeavouring to get alongside young people in a way that makes Jesus real to them – or, in the words of my colleague Terry Dunnell, in a way that 'enables young people to connect their story to the story of Jesus'. In the passage in Luke, Jesus' acceptance of the woman allowed him to appreciate the spiritual significance of her response to him and to affirm it. Furthermore, by holding her up as an example of love to the religious élite of his day, he showed that the 'poor' have a special place in God's heart. Maybe their desperation enables them to reach out to Jesus with a truer humility and a deeper desire to find him.

However, the spark of creativity and the impetus to write was ignited in me by my rereading Luke's Gospel and rediscovering the wonder of Jesus and his life. Passages that had once been merely interesting now became fascinating. Familiar stories took on new and deeper meanings. Every Bible study was exciting! I was like a child who had opened a box expecting to find a few boiled sweets; instead I found it stuffed full of Belgian chocolates. As I tasted each one, a whole range of exotic new flavours and sensations came flooding out. I must confess, though, that I had my favourites. My heart warmed as I read about Jesus meeting the blind and the lame, prostitutes and tax collectors, people with leprosy and beggars, widows and children. I was filled with compassion and praise as I saw him enable society's rejects to find not only acceptance and healing but a new friend and Lord.

As I read Luke, I was reminded of the way the Bridges team had tried to work with those at society's edge. I was greatly encouraged by the confirmation of my opinion at the time, which was that they were acting in sympathy with God's heart. Luke's Gospel was helping me to make connections between Jesus and my Bridges experience. In particular, closer study of the encounter between Jesus and the woman led me to pay special attention to verses 41–42, a part of the passage I had never taken much notice of before. This time I reflected deeply on the implications of what Jesus was saying (we will come back to this later, in chapter five).

The four Gospel writers – Matthew, Mark, Luke and John – look at Jesus from different perspectives, but each see someone who is compelling and with whom they can relate. Jesus had a remarkable ability to make connections with a variety of people. He loved, cared for and understood them. He was deeply committed to God and to them. Because of this, he established intimacy with them quickly and had the capacity to touch them at the deepest level. In Jesus, the divine became human, the supernatural became natural, the unobtainable became accessible, and the giver of life entered into life.

My final introduction is to Luke the physician, whose account I have featured in this book. It is no surprise that Luke, who gives such emphasis to Jesus' compassionate interaction with the poor, oppressed and marginalised, should be the one whose words so resonate with my Bridges experience and my heart. In the four Gospels, one out of every ten verses is about the poor, but in Luke the average is one out of seven.

So, the introductions are now complete; the story is set to begin. I am delighted to have this opportunity to tell you about Bridges, a truly remarkable project whose story deserves to be told. Of course, nothing is without fault, and if the project were to start again today some things would have to change (for example, guidelines on safe practice are now much more stringent). However, I should tell you that this story is written from a Christian perspective, with personal reflections on my own experience there. At Bridges, I was part of a team whose members each have their own unique story, their reasons for working there and their perspective on what effect it had on them. While it is my privilege to be able to share my own heart in this way, I can only give you a flavour of their experiences.

Jesus' life lit up my day-to-day working life in a special way, as well as illuminating the lives of the people he encountered. I hope passionately that this book will help those who, like me, are committed to following Jesus by building relationships with people at the edge, so that they too are drawn to him and desire to know more about him for themselves. This is an awesome challenge but one to which, I believe, Christians are called to respond.

For *Making Connections* to come alive for you as you read, may I invite you to:

- Put your everyday concerns and preconceptions to one side.

- Commit yourself to endeavouring to walk in the shoes of another, to listen and to learn.

- Sit at the feet of Jesus, and ask him to help you see the world through his loving eyes.

# Chapter 1

# ARRIVAL

*The Word became a human being...*

(John 1:14)

'Hatfield?!'

I switched the phone receiver to my left ear, just in case this changed what I was hearing.

'Yes. It's a project that seems to be in line with what you're generally looking for. But it will be very challenging!'

I paused to let the words sink in. I had applied to Community Service Volunteers to do a year's voluntary work, to test my suitability for a job in one of the helping professions and to gain some experience in the field. CSV placed volunteers all over the country and, having recently completed a degree in Sociology, I saw this as the next step towards independence. The uncertainty surrounding the location of my placement was a key part in the coming adventure. But Hatfield was only five miles from where I was living with my parents, so it held neither the mystique nor the romance associated with taking on a new challenge in unfamiliar territory far away from home. I felt that the wind had been taken out of my sails.

Thankfully, I carefully considered the suggestion from CSV. Somehow the words 'very challenging' lent some attraction. As long as I was careful to use my friends and family as a support and not a crutch, I thought, being close to them might have some advantages. This turned out to be a wise decision (and probably an inspired one). Going to the Bridges Project in Hatfield changed my life.

The other two volunteers at the project – Lorna and Shelley – had rooms in the hostel at Number 9A. Lorna showed me to my room at the top of the stairs in 9B, the drop-in centre. The room was an odd mixture. There was a single mattress on the floor, a dark brown wall-cupboard, a brightly painted rainbow above a bricked-up fireplace, and a chair by a small writing table. I walked to the window and looked out on a road, a mini-round-about, a bus stop and a few local shops. This was my new home.

At Lorna's suggestion, about an hour later I wandered next door to the hostel, where some residents were hanging around an open window at the back of her room. We chatted, checking each other out for a while. Then, as the light grew dim on a late October afternoon, I left to complete my unpacking. As I walked away, one of the group, Marcus, called out, 'See yer, *Christian.*' I continued walking so as to appear unmoved, but asked myself how Marcus could possibly already be aware of my faith, since I hadn't yet mentioned it to anyone. In our first real chat a few days later, Marcus admitted that calling someone 'Christian' was one of his ways of getting a reaction from the other person. Telling him that I actually was a Christian ensured that knowledge of my faith spread quickly. It was also the trigger for my first Bridges conversation about Jesus.

Marcus was one of the characters who feature prominently in my earliest memories of Bridges. When I began, he was approaching eighteen and had already had considerable contact with the project. Marcus constantly wore black jeans, a painted black leather jacket that was ripped in several places, and Doc Marten boots that came up to his calves. His hair was long but shaved at the sides – a Mohican style that was manipulated into vertical spikes on rare occasions. His healthily tanned complexion, brown eyes and winning smile ensured that he captured many admiring glances as well as attention. His dark features and attire, on the other hand, were symbolic of the more destructive side of his nature.

Tuesday evening at Bridges was swimming night and one of my responsibilities was to help Toby, a local volunteer, to take project users to the nearby pool. I soon realised that the hot chocolate and biscuits that always appeared on our return were our reward for personal sacrifice in the line of duty. The thought of them kept Tony and I going when either of us was receiving our fifteenth ducking of the night. One particular Tuesday, we were all sitting in the Bridges main room, enjoying our drinks, when a full plate of bourbons began to circulate. By the time the biscuits reached me, there was only one left. Seated opposite, a grinning Marcus was hastily pushing a quantity of the small, sweet, brown objects inside his leather jacket. I was annoyed; all my strongly held principles about fairness and sharing were offended. Many in the group had only enjoyed one solitary biscuit, and Marcus had not even gone swimming!

In a supervision session with Julie, the team leader, I mentioned my frustration at what had happened. She understood my feelings and talked through alternative strategies for next Tuesday. However, she also reminded me that this was an example of the strategies for survival many project users had developed: life had taught them that the plate of biscuits never came back; better, then, to grab as much as possible while it was available.

Another early incident involving Marcus happened on a night he saw me returning in the project car. Unbeknown to me, as I drove round to the garages, he gathered a large black garment around him and followed. The intense darkness, combined with his ability to creep silently, meant that I neither saw nor heard him climb onto the garage roof. When I emerged from parking the car, a dark, menacing swirl landed at my side, frightening me half to death. However, on discovering the phantom to be a smiling Marcus, my fear turned to nervous laughter. We walked back to Bridges relaxed and talking about the incident. Somehow I knew it was a positive sign that Marcus had chosen me as the victim of his ingenious prank.

CSV were right – Bridges was indeed a challenging placement. There was no gentle induction or warm-up period: almost as soon as I arrived I was rubbing shoulders with people whose life circumstances and experiences were so different from my own. At first it was difficult coming to terms with the many new situations and I felt very uncomfortable. The streetwise project users seemed far more adept than I at making the best of any new situation. They knew how to exploit my unfamiliarity with procedures or to push the boundaries of acceptable behaviour, to see how I would react. They also had a sixth sense that picked up any uncertainty or defensiveness on my part, and they frequently took advantage of this. But their quick-wittedness, developed through tough circumstances, helped my own sensitivity and sense of humour to become sharper. Nevertheless, to find myself so often feeling impatient, vulnerable and weak was painful and humbling. It sometimes seemed scant consolation for my growing self-awareness.

Several factors helped me not only to survive at Bridges but to become accepted and to go on to form many significant relationships there. First, the team of workers was excellent. Regular meetings ensured clear communication and decision-making. They also provided good opportunities for discussions on key parts of the project philosophy, which I would record in my working diary. Monthly training meetings supplemented this day-to-day learning with deeper, more reflective thinking. The presence of committed local volunteers brought other perspectives. Significantly, Bridges' close-knit team meant that difficult times were always shared. I rarely experienced feelings of isolation.

A second important feature was the regular supervisory session I had with Julie each week. This gave me space to say how I was coping, to discuss events that caused me pain or concern, and to grapple with some of the reasons why things happened as they did. The meeting was a source of support, learning and re-energising for me. I think I benefited through being honest about my lack of prior knowledge and experience, as it meant that I had an attitude of openness and was willing to learn from my mistakes.

Finally, I grew to have tremendous respect for the commitment of the team to the welfare of project users, and for the values that underpinned our working methods. It was encouraging, as a Christian, to know that I was part of a project which cared for disadvantaged people in a Christlike way (even though it would not have labelled itself a 'Christian' project). Before starting at Bridges I had feared that my efforts to be 'a good person' would be ridiculed. But I was surprised to discover that the wisest and best way to relate to project users, to influence them positively and gain their respect, was to treat them as closely as I could to the way I perceived Jesus would have done.

At the time, my appreciation of Jesus' example was instinctive; something within assured me that Bridges' work was honouring God. However, as I made time to read and reflect on Jesus' life, the profound nature of his earthly ministry truly came alive. As Luke's Gospel was illuminated for me, my gut feelings about Bridges were reinforced by greater insight.

I am filled with wonder that God actually sent Jesus – his only, precious and righteous Son – into the messiness and vulnerability of life on earth. And right from the start it is clear that his coming would turn the world upside down. Luke tells us that it was shepherds who were among the first to hear the news of his birth:

> ...the angel said to them, 'Don't be afraid! I am here with good news for you, which will bring great joy to all the people. This very day in David's town your Saviour was born – Christ the Lord.'
>
> *(Luke 2:10–11)*

Notice how the angel first points out that the good news is for 'all the people', but then adds '*your* Saviour was born'. The re-emphasis is there, I believe, because the shepherds might well have needed convincing that *they* were included. Shepherds were poor, unskilled men who spent many hours with their sheep on isolated hillsides. In the eyes of society, they had no prestige or respect and were often figures of fun. In Jesus' lifetime, shepherding was one of seven occupations that automatically deprived persons of Jewish civil and political rights (tax collectors were another). The angel's appearance to the shepherds was a sign that Jesus would identify with the poor, the despised and the marginalised.

By coming to earth in human likeness, Jesus was on a level with ordinary people; the divine Word became flesh and came to live among us, as one of us. People could see, smell, touch, taste and feel the integrity that shone out from him. Yet his exceptional qualities did not keep them at a distance. They were drawn to him. He was flesh and bone, and they could identify with him. He was real.

During my first months of living and working at Bridges, I was thrown into an unfamiliar environment. It felt as though my faith had, hitherto, been theoretical, untried and untested; but now, in the stark and pressured reality of daily life, it had to be proved. Individual verses became a challenge as well as a source of inspiration. The earliest of entries in my Bridges diary says of one hostel resident, Leonard:

> Do I love Leonard, or is he a nuisance to me, bothering me ... Love is not ill-mannered or selfish or irritable; love does not keep a record of wrongs ... Love never gives up; and its faith, hope, and patience never fail (1 Corinthians 13:5,7).

Any opportunities that came to tell the story of my experiences to interested Christian friends were greatly valued, as were their prayers. I managed to keep my head up, aware of my responsibility to be a positive influence and a faithful follower of Jesus. However, I was often most aware of my inadequacy, defensiveness and impatience, and my wish simply to get through another day. Nevertheless, I knew that I was in the right place, and increasingly convinced that God's desire for us is to live for him in the nitty-gritty of life. If, as Christians, we seek to make meaningful connections with others, they will need the opportunity to see Jesus in us, in our characters, in our actions, in the way we live our lives. This can only be done if we are close enough for this to be noticed. At Bridges I had to overcome my inclination to be reserved and to want to communicate faith from a safe distance. If we are to be faithful to God's example in sending Jesus, then our words need to 'become flesh', embodied in us – warts and all.

## Think about
*   Read John 1:1–5,14; Philippians 2:5–7. (You might like to use the Bible passages as a starting point for prayer or to reflect on the following.)

- Jesus left the security of his place with God and came close to ordinary people, as a human being.

- Identify an environment where you are seeking to build relationships away from the security of Christian fellowship, where your faith has to be seen to be real.

- As you seek to make connections with people at the edge, will your primary focus of contact be at work, at college, in the local community, or with a particular group of friends or fellow members of a club?

- Is God calling you, individually or as a church, to follow Jesus in developing relationships with people who are at the edge of mainstream society (eg the homeless)?

# Chapter 2

# CONTACT

*The Word ... lived among us.*

(John 1:14)

The first time I sat in the main room at Bridges, I felt uncomfortable and self-conscious: uncomfortable because I was sitting with strangers in unfamiliar surroundings; self-conscious because occupying any of the armchairs located along the walls of this square-shaped room necessarily compelled its incumbent to face the others who were present. So, trying hard to look relaxed, I settled back and set about studying the room's features. Most of the walls were covered in posters, and for a while I was lost in details about healthy teeth. A radio-stereo sat quietly in one corner, and opposite, in the privacy of a cubby-hole below the stairs, someone was using a phone. I tried to look friendly but not over-eager. It seemed better to remain quiet rather than risk a nauseatingly inappropriate topic of conversation. In the absence of voices, my grip on the arms of the chair remained very firm. Who were the others sitting around me? What were they thinking about me? And where on earth were the other workers?

As the months passed, the main room at Bridges became less of a daunting experience. However, it retained its capacity to challenge and always represented something deeply significant about the job at hand. It was not entirely accidental that on this initial visit I found myself in what was the focal point of the drop-in centre without the support of other workers – it was the first element of my training. All workers needed to become comfortable just sitting in the company of project users if they were to survive.

My new role at Bridges seemed to centre around a number of practical tasks:

- Taking hostel bedding and residents' clothing to the launderette.

- Collecting family visitors to the drop-in centre and taking them home at the end of the day.

- Delivering messages to homes, local agencies or professionals, as and when they were needed.

- Meeting hostel residents on 'dole money' day to collect their rent.

As I began to fulfil these tasks, it became clear that there were other elements involved. Thursday's rent collection from the post office is a good example. I was not simply there to collect money; I was also there to spend time with any residents who might value some company. Those still awaiting their first cheque would join me for a Coke or a coffee. Sometimes a young person would come by, having cashed their giro, and pay for the drinks. Then we would drift round the shops, taking in the local record store which helped us to develop an awareness of our mutual tastes in music. Some residents would buy jeans, tee-shirts or fashionable items of jewellery. They appreciated my presence as an interested observer or when the change in their appearance was noticed and complimented. Over time, I developed a small-scale banking system whereby some residents would give me a small proportion of Thursday's money to keep until the following Monday and Tuesday when funds had run out. So, in lots of small ways, the post office trip was a trigger for building relationships.

> For ... people who have felt abandoned, there is only one reality that will bring them back to life; an authentic, tender and faithful relationship. They must discover that they are loved ... Only then will they discover they are worthwhile. And to love is not to do something; it is to be with them. It is to rejoice in their presence; it is to give them confidence in the value of their being; it is to listen to them and to their needs and desires; it is to help them

find their confidence in themselves and in their capacity to please, to do, to serve, and to be useful.

*(Jean Vanier)*[1]

Although it was rarely a smooth process, time spent with project users clearly built up our mutual awareness and trust. I became more comfortable living among those to whom I was committing my time, and I was learning for myself how, as workers, we were principally there to build relationships and to have a positive influence on the lives of others through getting alongside them and working with them. This was a key element that prompted me to rethink my intention to use the CSV placement as a stepping-stone to a career in probation work. In terms of status and emphasis, it had seemed an appropriate path for someone with a degree, who had particularly enjoyed studying Criminology. At Bridges, however, I encountered the antagonism which a number of project users felt towards their welfare professionals. Some had a social worker who appeared indifferent to their situation, perhaps through lack of time; others were compelled by the courts to see a probation officer who seemed to make no positive difference to their lives. For many, the painful experiences of their childhood or teenage years meant that any worker faced an uphill struggle establishing a positive relationship with them. Some professionals did overcome these obstacles and proved effective, but it was evident that the role of probation officer might distance me from many of the people I hoped to help. This impression was reinforced by the reactions of those who met their clients at Bridges. A few strode into the main room, happily joined in the mêlée, and would even hold the child of someone they knew. A great many, however, hovered uncomfortably in the confined space of the hallway, just inside the front door. Perhaps it was our reputation or the intensity of the main-room atmosphere which made them wary. Whichever, it was noticeable how significant was the potential distance between professional and client.

In chapter one, I explained how going to Bridges convinced me that if Christians are to make meaningful connections with people at the edge of society, they need to get close enough to them so as to 'be Jesus' to them, though this will probably be an uncomfortable experience at times. Following Christ's example involves getting alongside others and working with them in a way that will reassure and empower them. Looking at Jesus in the light of my Bridges experience draws out two aspects to this. First, Jesus said to his disciples, 'I will ask the Father, and he will give you another Counsellor who will stay with you for ever' (John 14:16). R T Kendall comments on this:

> Now this word translated 'counsellor' is the Greek word 'paracletos'; it means literally 'one who comes alongside'. Now the fact that Jesus said, 'He will give you another Counsellor' shows that that is what he had been up till then.[2]

Jesus' words to the disciples affirm our view on the position and the manner in which he worked with others. For me, however, being alongside others at Bridges was one thing; but comparisons with Jesus swiftly broke down in the area of my actual working practice. The memory of clumsy confrontations, missed opportunities to listen and to share, the barrier of shyness or embarrassment, and words that closed doors rather than opening them, remains uncomfortably clear.

Let us look at a different translation of the verse that heads this chapter, to draw out my next point: 'The Word ... moved into the neighbourhood' (from Eugene Peterson's *The Message*). One of the fundamental challenges of being at Bridges was to become comfortable just being in 'the neighbourhood' – something that many visitors found difficult and few visiting professionals seemed to achieve. When we set out to make connections with others, setting up home 'in the neighbourhood' is immensely significant both symbolically and practically. What I find amazing about Jesus is that here he is, the Son of God, with all the status in the world, yet he enabled ordinary people to feel so loved and welcomed they could bring their needs, share of themselves and ask him questions. Those around him felt that he understood their deepest hurts and heartfelt wishes. Much of the answer lies in the choices he made about where he spent his time, who he spent his time with, and how he conducted his ministry.

The idea of getting too close to people at the edge might seem disconcerting or uncomfortable. Maybe for you alarm bells begin to ring about the dangers of worldliness and compromising Christian values. I think we are influenced in these things by our view of the nature of the Christian's relationship to society and culture. Broadly speaking, there seem to be four perspectives. At the furthest extreme is the view that the world is entirely corrupt and Christians need to separate from it completely. A second, less black-and-white view still sees everyday culture as unrelated or irrelevant to how the Christian faith is lived out; thus the sacred and secular activities of life remain apart. At the other extreme is the opinion that most contemporary cultural life represents something positive; Christians simply need to add the spiritual icing to a societal cake that is full of excellent ingredients. These three ideas can be summarised respectively as rejecting, remaining separate from, and embracing the world.

I believe there is a fourth approach, which is embodied in Jesus. He lived among people and actively engaged with the society around him, but remained constantly aware of the parts that need to change. He was not afraid to play his part directly or to encourage the reshaping of society in a Christlike way. Put simply, Christ transforms the world.

Two incidents at the start of Jesus' public ministry provide good examples of this. In John 2:1–11, we read that Jesus attended a wedding in Cana, Galilee, where the wine runs out during the festivities. His mother, Mary, asks him for help. With the servants on hand to assist with the practicalities, Jesus turns earthenware jugs of water into good quality wine. Then, in Luke 5:1–11, Jesus invites Peter to recast his fishing nets, despite the fact that Peter and his colleagues have laboured all the previous night with no success. The resulting catch is so huge, extra help is required to haul it ashore. In both instances we find Jesus in the middle of a familiar scene from the local culture – a wedding feast and the workplace of Galilean fishermen. It is here, in the midst of everyday life, that Jesus begins to reveal his extraordinary and transforming power, and to make a difference: 'you have saved the best wine until now' (John 2:10); 'they ... caught such a large number of fish that the nets were about to break' (Luke 5:6).

I was once part of a group of Christian men brought together by Ambassadors In Sport to tour three countries, using football as a means to share the gospel. During the trip, the group stayed in an Austrian town for two days, where the minister of a local church was our principal contact. At the same time, a group of German students, who had already been based there for ten days, were building up to the climax of their local mission. They had invited everyone in the town to an evening at the church, where a Christian film was shown and a guest speaker shared the gospel message. The evening went smoothly and the church was full, but later it emerged that only two of the guests were completely new contacts: the rest were from local churches.

The following day, the Ambassadors team played at the town's football ground against the local team, for whom the church minister was making a guest appearance. The locals kindly organised a barbecue to follow the game, enabling us to meet players and friends from the club. We performed our tour song, exchanged club colours, and one of our players shared the story of how he became a Christian. Then we all sat down to share a meal. Before long I got talking to their goalkeeper, Hans (or was it Hands?!). He told me that many in Austrian society were disillusioned with Christianity because of the apparent hypocrisy of powerful church leaders, and that he himself had suffered because of a strict religious upbringing: both these things were barriers to faith for him. I encouraged him to reconsider by looking afresh at the story of Jesus. On another table sat a young student named Christian. As we chatted, it soon became obvious that here was a deep intellectual thinker intent on resolving all possible questions about the Christian faith before he would consider making a personal response. In response, I told him some of the very tangible ways in which God had positively affected my life.

Afterwards, when the Ambassadors team gathered together, players were queuing up to recount a variety of encouraging stories from the evening. There was a strong feeling that many people had shown much more than just a polite interest in Jesus. The local minister said he had carried out more effective outreach in that one evening than during the whole of his two years in the town. 'If only we could come back tomorrow,' someone said, as we left in a mood of great excitement and deep gratitude to God.

Bearing in mind that there are limitations to very short-term work, there is a marked contrast between the apparent effectiveness of the football team's experience compared with that of the student group. The Ambassador's project benefited from focusing on football, a cultural activity that transcends national boundaries. Playing against the local team ensured that visitors and locals alike could show off their skills and abilities, and give their competitive instincts full reign. The post-match gathering was a response to an invitation from the local team, and we met in an environment where they felt at home. Sitting around tables, eating, was conducive to sharing informally. All this made it possible to get alongside others and talk about Jesus, the reason for our visit. In fact, I find it easy to imagine Jesus there as one of those sitting and chatting with us.

The Concise Oxford Dictionary defines an ambassador as an accredited diplomat sent by a State on a mission to, or as its permanent representative in, a foreign country; and a representative or promoter of a specified thing. The NIV translation uses the word in 2 Corinthians, where the apostle Paul describes the Christian's role in bringing the gospel to the world: 'We are therefore Christ's ambassadors, as though God were making his appeal through us' (5:20). As the same translation says in verse 14, 'Christ's love compels us' to share the love of Jesus. But as well as compelling, it also propels us: not content for those outside to come to us, or to wait for them to become more comfortable or acceptable to be with, Jesus calls us to go out into the everyday world that people inhabit and to come alongside those he guides us to encounter. This is one of the foundations we must lay as we seek to make connections with others. It is from this position that we find the potential to build significant and meaningful relationships with others. From here, Jesus is able to convey his love, show something of himself and reveal his ability to transform situations as we allow him to work in and through our lives.

## Think about

- Read John 1:10–14; Philippians 2:5–7. (You might like to use the Bible passages as a starting point for prayer or to reflect on the following.)

- Jesus left his elevated place with God and came to earth. He lived alongside people in such a way that they felt loved, accepted and understood.

- As a Christian, you have identified a particular context (at work, at college, in the community, with friends or fellow club-members) where you are seeking to build relationships. Are you spending time just hanging out, so that you can get to know others and they you?

- Do you feel that you are creating situations where social status can be forgotten and/or you can get beyond roles? Informal venues, meeting out of normal hours, and conversations that provide opportunities for deeper sharing will all be helpful.

- Jesus spent time with people at the edge of society. Do you, individually or as a church, need to create circumstances in which this happens?

- However it is done, try to ensure that this involves you going to the edge in some way, and that real love and serving others form the basis for building relationships, not charity.

## Notes

1   Jean Vanier, *The Challenge of L'Arche*, Darton, Longman and Todd, 1982, p2.

2   R T Kendall, *The Holy Spirit and Forgiveness*, Walking With Jesus (audiotape series), Scripture Union, 1992.

# Chapter 3

# DISCOVERY

*Before suggesting solutions, however good
they may be, the helper must first discover the
beauty of the wounded person, hidden under
the ugliness and violence. In effect, love is not
primarily to do something, but it is to reveal to
that person his or her value, not only through
listening or tenderness but also through
competence and faithful commitment.*

(Writer unknown)

Driving along that morning, I had a tremendous feeling of well-being. It was a bright October day and the glistening sun illuminated the golden leaves on scores of horse chestnut trees lined up along each side of the road, their branches joined to form an archway through this part of Thetford Forest. Empty chestnut shells were strewn amid the tree trunks, and they took me back to my childhood quest for conkers: eager young arms throwing heavy sticks into trees and the joy of finding the places where the treasures had already fallen to the ground. Discovering those glistening red conkers was always more exciting than using them!

As I reminisced, it occurred to me that, with a little imagination, we could compare people to horse chestnuts. The outer surface is the protective skin – sometimes worn away, sometimes not fully developed, sometimes prickly. Inside sits the shiny conker in a delicate white casing – the vulnerable and sensitive layers of our lives protecting the precious core. Some conkers easily burst free from their skins. Others remain inside despite falling to the ground. They go unnoticed because there are lots of shiny conkers around; or they are neglected because of their shabby appearance or because it is too much trouble to extricate them. With the prickly ones, great care is needed to get to the conker without too much harm to oneself.

At Bridges, discovering 'conkers' took commitment and patience, but time spent with project users challenged my impressions, unearthed some remarkable stories and expanded the perspective I had of those I was alongside. Experiences with two particular individuals stand out in my memory. The first person could be described as troublesome and prickly, the other as shabby and worn.

## Leonard

He came to Bridges as a sixteen-year-old with a reputation. Leonard had been kicked out of a number of children's homes and had spent time in a youth custody centre. This cut no ice with the older, established residents when he arrived, and a subdued Leonard remained the junior hostel occupant for some while. However, it was not long before his confidence grew. Leonard was a live-wire who got up to a number or tricks, given half a chance – or less. He could be charming and immensely funny. He could also, we discovered, be difficult and tiresome.

One day Leonard asked me if he could have some money from the safe. This was a social services grant which was earmarked for clothing and could only be spent on an organised trip. After checking on the facts via the phone, I reminded Leonard of this and closed the office door, leaving him outside it. Almost immediately, I felt it rattle heavily with the weight of two heavy kicks. Like many, he frequently pushed against the boundaries upheld by workers and grappled with how to express feelings of frustration and anger. In contrast, just a few weeks later, a group from Bridges took an Easter trip to Hyde Park. In the midday sunshine we walked round the Serpentine in search of boats to hire. We had gone quite a way when someone spotted them still a long way away on the other side of the water. Just at that moment, amidst all the moans and groans, Leonard politely asked me if I could miraculously part the waters and save them the extra walk! Humour like that relaxes everyone.

Leonard and I gradually developed a good relationship, but it took many, many months of consistent time spent patiently alongside each other. What helped me considerably were the moments when his guard was lowered and I glimpsed another side of Leonard. The first time this happened, six months after I began at Bridges, was one of the most memorable I experienced with anyone. At eleven o'clock one night, Lorna, the worker on hostel duty, knocked on my door and asked if I could collect her backup worker, Lisa. There had been an incident involving residents on the way back from the local pub and extra help was required. In the car, Lisa gave more details. Leonard had met his dad and brother for a drink at lunch time; then, in the evening he had bumped into fellow resident Andy at the Red Lion. For some reason, during their walk back Andy had hit Leonard. Andy's short fuse, Leonard's capacity to irritate and a significant quantity of alcohol were such a potentially dangerous cocktail that the incident came as no great surprise.

Back at Bridges, Lisa sat Leonard down and chatted with him. I retreated to the kitchen, to make three hot drinks. By the time I returned Leonard was sobbing at Lisa's side. I sat quietly in the corner and listened as parts of his story subsequently emerged. Leonard was one of about a dozen children. He was very fond of his dad, but, due to a poor relationship with his step-mum, was generally not allowed to visit, let alone live, at the family home. Two Christmases ago, for the first time in years, he had been given permission to come to the house on Christmas Day, but only in order to exchange presents. Last year, his step-mum had signed his present for the first time. In those few minutes, all Leonard's sharpness, cockiness and bravado fell away, and I listened to a painfully hurt young man sharing the reality of his family life, and his desperate longing for one that was different.

This was a key moment for me. By spending considerable time with people like Leonard, I became very aware that there was far more to others' lives than I might otherwise have known. Each project user was the holder of a biography whose chapters were so complex and tragic they were still having a powerful impact on his or her everyday life. Appreciating this developed my understanding and increased my commitment to the people at Bridges. Having had the privilege to listen to some of Leonard's story that night, I could no longer look at him in the same way.

## Clive

The voice on the phone was familiar. Cheryl, from Shelter, was wondering if I could give someone advice about lodgings. She suggested we both go to meet him at his present accommodation – a shack in a wood five miles away. A number of large private houses backed onto those woods and the 'woodman', as I call him, had formerly lived with his parents in one of them. However, conflict in the family had reached such a level that the parents had taken out an injunction to remove their son. They then moved away, and it was the new occupants of the house who had contacted Shelter. Along with other residents, they were worried about the presence of someone living in the woods who was said to have an aggressive manner. There were also fears that he might be tempted to break into his former home. And, more charitably, there was some concern for his welfare.

Cheryl and I drove to the woodland area on a damp December morning, and were joined by Liz, a representative from a local mental health charity, who was familiar with the family circumstances. The three of us, with Liz in her wheelchair, progressed slowly through soggy ground towards the shack. The wooden structure was large and impressively made, and could easily have been concealing its architect since there was no one in sight when we arrived. Nevertheless, I introduced myself so that my voice would be familiar when I called again.

The second visit took place on Boxing Day, about a fortnight later. It was early evening before I managed to find a suitable gap in the family festivities, so the woods were already dark and eerie as, with a black bag (a Bridges food parcel) slung over my shoulder, I climbed over a garden fence and into the grounds of the house nearest the shack. If any passers-by had seen me then, they would almost certainly have called the police. However, I was more concerned about who might be in the woods.

I was just beginning to feel rather apprehensive, when a figure appeared in front of me. Startled, I hastily identified myself, explained the purpose of my visit and proffered the black bag. It was accepted with apparent gratitude and, as the woodman drew closer to take it, I could just make out a crumpled jacket with a hood and long beard. He suggested that I return by a less dangerous route and offered to show me the way. I blindly followed the silent, torch-bearing figure, with fantasies of abduction invading my imagination, and was rather relieved to reach the road a few minutes later. We shook hands and said, 'Happy Christmas.'

Around the New Year there was a spell of freezing weather and Liz became so concerned about the circumstances of the woodman that she called in the police. He was admitted to hospital in a very poor state of health and was later transferred to the psychiatric wing for assessment.

At the beginning of February, during a hectic late afternoon at Bridges, a colleague informed me that someone had come to see me. I found my caller and suggested we sit down away from the bustle of activity. I looked across at my visitor. He was a tall, slim man with red hair and a moustache. He introduced himself as Clive Mallon. I shall never forget the next few moments. As he talked, it became obvious that the frightening, featureless figure from the woods was now sitting in front of me, a friendly, smiling human being. Clive explained that he was presently still in hospital, but would soon be leaving to be housed in a local council bedsit. He had wanted to find me to say 'Thank you'.

I wonder how the residents of the houses near Clive's shack would have reacted if they had met him that day? Sadly, to them, he probably remains a sinister or curious character who features only in anecdotal stories. However, in that moment of recognition as I was introduced to Clive, someone began to emerge from behind the disfiguring coverings of a wooden shack and the anonymity of a pulled-up hood. How easily I could have forgotten about the woodman after the first visit, had it not been near Christmas. As it turned out, the gift of the food parcel gave me the opportunity to see beyond the exterior, to greet a real person. It was a privilege to meet Clive Mallon.

There are similarities between Clive and the man described in Luke 8:26–39 (you may want to read the Bible story at this point). Both are unusual figures, living aloof from the communities of which they were formerly a part, and to varying degrees they both appear frightening to others.

As Jesus steps onto the shore of Lake Galilee, the man emerges from the burial caves, scarcely clothed and probably with chains hanging from his wrists and ankles. His only human contact is with those who keep him chained up. The marginalised, alienated figure seems more akin to a wild animal than a human being. No wonder the local people are shocked and fearful when they later see him clothed, composed and talking to Jesus. What has happened to him?

The man's demonic possession is a particular need requiring especially skilful help. While acknowledging this, the story remains an excellent illustration of how Jesus can unearth the precious 'conker' inside those who come to him, and bring healing and wholeness to the scarred, ostracised and despised.

Despite Jesus' example and those formative experiences at Bridges, I still regularly find myself making negative assumptions about others based on their appearance or because of an anti-social or irritating trait they have. I want, therefore to outline three thoughts which may help all of us to build more effective relationships with others, especially those at the edge.

## Maintain your commitment to the welfare of others

'Jesus, Son of the Most High God! What do you want with me? I beg you, don't punish me!' (Luke 8:28).

In the face of words like these, containing as they do a disconcerting level of insight, challenge and fear, it would be hard to stay unperturbed. But throughout the encounter Jesus retains his focus on the man's welfare and deals with his particular needs – a feature of his overall ministry.

When we get beneath the surface of a person we will usually discover a sea of needs. We must learn how to interpret those needs correctly, as Jesus did. Jesus wasn't

turned off by our needs – even needs wrongly met –
because they revealed something about the person.

*(Rebecca Pippert)*[1]

This quote reminds me of a helpful phrase I noted down during
one of my first team meetings at Bridges: 'Our job is not to police
but to find out how people tick'. Our aim was to build relationships that helped others to develop, not to retain control so that
everything ran smoothly. Any insights about people gained
through circumstance or time were to be used sensitively and
wisely, and always with the welfare of those people in mind. As
a result, our ability to make connections with others was significantly helped.

## Always remember that there is a human face

Jesus was able to identify the source of the problems afflicting
'Mob' (or 'Legion' in the NIV). He recognised that this was a
man possessed and not a wild animal who needed to be tamed. In
the face of shouts, seizures, chains and an unkempt appearance,
Jesus never forgot the hidden human face of the real person.
Meeting Clive Mallon revealed to me the human face behind the
upturned hood and wooden shack. Leonard's story helped me to
appreciate the complex background to some peoples lives. Both
encounters helped to develop my tolerance and understanding of
unusual and challenging behaviour. Dave Andrews here empha-
sises the importance of love:

The more we truly love our fellow human beings, the
more likely we are to be affected by a sense of their
immense worth when we see them most scarred by their
background, environment or experience. So much the
more generously, then, will we be led to reach out to them
and to bring to light the treasure buried and obscured
within them. For we all have treasure within us.

*(Dave Andrews)*[2]

I am not sure if unearthing treasure at Bridges created a spring of love within me, but I know that it unlocked a greater depth of compassion, and I believe that I caught just a taste of the depth of love for the disadvantaged which lies within God's heart. I am not talking here about feeling pity ('Oh, poor them!') or some kind of relief ('Thank goodness it wasn't me!). In fact, quite the opposite – I was beginning to discover a human bond of empathy within, which had perhaps been formed in the process of living through my own moments of pain and isolation. I was comprehending a commonality beneath the surface of all our lives: an emotional connection at a deeper level, which is something we can build on with others even when our lives seem unconnected in most other ways.

## Keep believing in people

Jesus never seems helpless or overwhelmed in the face of great human need. He is not intimidated or repelled by the demonic presence within Mob because he has the power and authority to deal with it. His faith and confidence in his divine ability to bring about change means that he never considers Mob to be beyond hope.

On a human level, I am pleased that Bridges had a positive approach both to its work and the project users. The underlying belief was that everyone had potential, and the team was united in its optimistic approach to what they could achieve. Bridges had a scheme in which members of the local community donated furniture for which they no longer had a use. Bridges then collected and stored it until someone known to be in need, or the project itself, found a home for it. In a similar way, many viewed the project as a place for young people who were rejects from the system; but we accepted them, worked with them and always saw their potential to have worthwhile lives. Because the project had long-term contact with individuals, we could draw confidence from and point to visible evidence of positive change in those still living close at hand. Bridges was committed to working with everyone they could, and was determined to show that no one should ever be written off.

At the end of the story in Luke chapter 8, the man wants to join

Jesus and the disciples. Whatever his reasons for preferring to send him home to tell his story, Jesus is willing to use this somewhat unlikely character in God's purposes. So, looking past our first impressions to see someone's potential, or glimpsing beneath the surface to find the hidden treasure, also means believing in people's ability to contribute spiritually, to be used by God.

Jesus' encounter with Mob and my own relationships with people like Leonard and Clive, lead me to suggest that, in making connections, we are asking God to work through us in such a way that people at the edge can sense us conveying three messages:

- 'I hear you, and I will be sensitive to what you have to tell me. Nothing shared will affect my ongoing commitment to you.'

- 'I will keep believing in you and your capacity for personal development.'

- 'I value you and wish to affirm your potential to contribute something of value to others.'

Maybe, through prayer and the work of God's Holy Spirit, the hearts of those to whom we are committed in this way will begin to realise that they can insert Jesus' name instead of ours. Consequently, the received messages will be:

- 'Jesus hears me, accepts me, believes in me and values me.'

Once this begins to happen, it opens up the exciting possibility that the person will ultimately get to the point of saying to Jesus:

- 'I want to have a relationship with you for myself. Thank you for loving me. I know you have a meaningful role for me and I want to be a part of your team. What do I have to do?'

## Think about

* Read 2 Corinthians 5:16; 1 Samuel 16:7; Matthew 25:31–40. (You might like to use the Bible passages as a starting point for prayer or to reflect on the following.)

* Jesus was willing to meet everyone. He was not repelled by the appearance and manner of people like the demon-possessed man, or intimidated by their great needs.

* Jesus' depth of compassion and insight helped him to see the hidden human face of those society had pushed aside or ignored. If you or your church are seeking to work with people at the edge, look for the human face of those you are meeting, but do so with sensitivity and respect. Be wise about deciding when more specialist help is required.

* Have you been thinking about how to ensure that there is time to build real relationships within the context in which you have chosen to operate? Always remember that each person has a unique life story and this will have a bearing on the way they present themselves. Remembering your own vulnerable times should help you to love and respect others.

* Be aware that first impressions are deceptive and dismissing others is foolish. Stay open to people – God often enables us to build significant relationships with someone unexpected.

## Notes

1 Rebecca Pippert, *Out of the Saltshaker: Evangelism as a way of life*, Inter-Varsity Press, 1980, p119.

2 Dave Andrews, 'Mary and the caring and sharing community', *Grow Comes of Age*, C Keogh (ed), Grow, Sydney, 1979, p40; in Andrews, *Building a Better World*, Lion, 1996, p89.

*Chapter 4*

# SPACE

*Therefore, healing means, first of all, the
creation of an empty space where those who
suffer can tell their story to someone who can
listen with real attention.*

(Henri Nouwen)[1]

The tourist bus was full. Knees quietly jostled for a comfortable position. The heat of the day, and the contented anticipation of a visit to Chitwan National Park in Southern Nepal, was enough to ensure that I dozed off. As we slowed in the approach to our destination and then shuddered to a halt, my peaceful slumber ended. I stirred slowly, safe in the assurance that our group's lack of accommodation would be resolved quickly and easily upon arrival. But we did not anticipate the traders who greeted us as we stepped from the vehicle into the midday sun. Almost instantly, we were besieged by a sea of pleading faces, dramatic gestures and imploring voices, as the local tourist industry went into overdrive. Everyone was endeavouring to claim the predominant place in our attentions. How could we possibly hear what a single trader had to offer, let alone carefully consider all?! And how could we justify favouring one lodge when each one so desperately needed the business? It was too much for me. I retreated in the face of a baking hot sun, unfamiliar surroundings and an overwhelming crowd, to find some quieter, personal space, leaving the others to deal with the maelstrom.

Jesus often found himself the focus of an expectant crowd, and he wins my admiration for the cool and remarkable way in which he responded to them. I wonder what the waiting crowd in Luke 8:40 were hoping for from him? (At this point you may like to read Luke 8:40–48, the focus of this chapter, or up to verse 56 to complete the story). Perhaps he would tell an intriguing story, say something wise, or ridicule the religious leaders? Maybe he would perform a miracle!

As everyone waits, a temple official named Jairus comes and falls at Jesus' feet, begging him to come to his house to heal his twelve-year-old daughter who is dying. However, also in the crowd is a woman who has suffered from chronic bleeding for twelve years, and who sees in Jesus a potential source of help for her desperate situation. Surreptitiously, she reaches out and touches his cloak. At once her bleeding stops. Jesus feels the power go out from him and asks, 'Who touched me?' When no one steps forward, Peter bravely asks what many are thinking: dozens of people are pressing in on Jesus and could have touched him – what does he mean? What about the waiting Jairus, for whom every passing minute threatens the life of his daughter? But Jesus refuses to budge. He persists in his quest to discover the answer to his question. Why is he so determined?

- Was he simply curious?

- Did he want to confirm that the woman's action had actually made a difference?

- Did he want to reassure her that her action had been acceptable and that she did not need to hide from him?

- Did he want to introduce himself, and confirm that his power and identity were linked?

- Did he sense, through the prompting of the Holy Spirit, that he needed to meet the woman?

Without discussing the comparative merits of these explanations, it is clear that Jesus considered his initial contact with the woman to be incomplete. Power had gone out from him, a connection had definitely been made, but it was somehow unfinished. Only after the woman has stepped forward and told him her story was he happy to let her go. This chapter focuses on how Bridges enabled me to discover the significance of this process.

In chapter three, we acknowledged how easy it is to dismiss other people because of something about them. The woman who touched Jesus was a person whom others would certainly have avoided or shunned. In the culture of the day, women had little status as it was; but for one who suffered from persistent bleeding there was the great shame of her physical condition making her ceremonially unclean (Lev 15:25–27). Within the Mishnah, the Hebrew holy law, seventy-nine paragraphs were devoted to regulations concerning menstruation, so closely was this physical state observed. Anyone who made contact with a woman in this condition, or with her belongings, required formal washing before they were restored to a state of ritual purity. No wonder the woman hesitated before admitting her actions and the illness that prompted them.

> There in front of everybody, she told him why she had
> touched him and how she had been healed at once.
>
> *(Luke 8:47)*

> The woman realised what had happened to her, so she
> came, trembling with fear, knelt at his feet, and told him
> the whole truth.
>
> *(Mark 5:33)*

Jesus knew that it was important to let the woman share 'the whole truth' of her story – the social estrangement and religious stigma as well as the twelve-year search for relief. The significance of standing alongside people in this way is explained by Henri Nouwen:

> Those who do not run away from our pains but touch them
> with compassion, bring healing and new strength. The
> paradox indeed is that the beginning of healing is in the
> solidarity with the pain.[2]

We all value finding a place where we can feel safe enough to be open about ourselves to someone who is sincerely interested and committed to our well-being. Let us briefly revisit the encounter between Leonard and Lisa, which I mentioned in the previous chapter.

When Lisa decided to come to the project that night, her immediate task was to help Lorna get everyone peacefully off to bed after an eventful evening. When, however, she perceived that Leonard might need to talk, Lisa was able to set the task aside and give him the space to talk. She had already established a relationship of trust with him, but a significant encounter only took place because Lisa created a genuine opportunity for sharing, for listening and for a meaningful connection to be made.

As someone new to the project, I lacked the established trust, self-confidence or the skill to be in Lisa's position that night, but over time I learnt to enable similar encounters to occur. One of the most significant means by which I developed one-to-one conversational skills was as co-ordinator for the Bridges lodgings scheme. Bridges had a permanent advertisement in the local paper which read: 'Homely lodgings wanted, ring XXXXX.' After discussion with Julie, we decided to improve the effectiveness of the service. Instead of simply noting down the details of respondents, I visited all the potential landlords/ ladies. As soon as local agencies like social services and the Citizen's Advice Bureau heard about our newly improved scheme, the referrals of homeless young people significantly increased. Over five years, about 300 16–35 year-olds spoke to me, and approximately 70 were found lodgings.

My first few visitors still come to mind because the interview process was completely new and untried. I attempted to be polite and thorough, always offering a drink and finding a quiet place in which to talk. Sometimes I knew at once that immediate help would not be available, for example if my visitor was male and the only available lodgings wanted a female. But it was always worth taking the details in case appropriate accommodation was phoned in during the next few days. However, as the scheme matured, I began to take longer talking to the young people I met. Often I was the next agency that was being visited after other negative responses. In these cases, the least I could do was spend time listening and taking an interest in the details of their situation. Most of all, I began to see that the process of creating space and committing myself to listen had an intrinsic value. Inadvertently, I was discovering the positive nature of listening.

With this in mind, I want to use an article by Joan Searle to highlight three ways in which creating space to listen is so valuable.[3]

1    'Letting off steam is a necessary measure from time to time, but it is impossible to do so satisfactorily unless someone is prepared to be sympathetic. The person who will listen helps to create a safety-valve for the pent-up emotions of the speaker.'

Most of the young people I met accepted the invitation to talk about the situation they were in and how they had come to be there. Their stories were often characterised by the pain of family conflict and relational breakdown, or the uncertainty of temporary housing situations with its accompanying disruption to employment and income. Occasionally I became very watchful, sensing that the interviewee was feeding me a line; but for the vast majority, the space and time to share was genuinely appreciated.

2    'The listener can also become a useful sounding-board, against which the speaker can project his ideas, the verbalising of beliefs and concepts is an important process in their clarification. Often it is not until they have been voiced that one can get a true picture of one's thoughts, for to hear one's ideas aloud and possibly restated by the listener, is to experience them in a new light.'

Offering a listening ear gives someone the opportunity to tell his or her story. As the actions, circumstances and reactions are pieced together for the ears of the hearer, the teller is able to make sense of what might previously have been perceived as a haphazard collection of events and, in the process, discover more about himself. Sometimes the storyteller will need encouragement to share or a question from the listener to aid clarification. So, for example, a young person might say, 'My step-dad's a nightmare. He's about to chuck me out.' This statement could be taken at face value, but experience at Bridges had shown me the importance of following it up with a question such as '*How* is he a nightmare?' Simple explorations like these can deepen the understanding of both teller and listener. They may also be a way of opening the door to a solution.

Creating space to listen with care and understanding became a significant aspect of my Bridges experience. It was humbling to see how the young people coped with difficult circumstances. The callous actions of some families, and the inflexibility and lack of provision in the welfare benefits system, often angered me. Most of all, hearing their stories helped me to sense something of what it is like to be homeless or threatened with homelessness. If we can remain open, this sort of listening sharpens our understanding and deepens our compassion.

3    'To listen attentively to someone is to convey certain
      attitudes to the person concerned. You are saying to him
      in fact that you have time for him, that he is worth your
      spending time, and that what he says is of value and
      deserves to be taken seriously ... in the case of the
      unloved and unwanted person such an experience can be
      of major importance.'

In providing real space and time to listen, we are saying that we value someone. I suspect that my willingness to listen was partly inspired by my experience of supervision. From the start, I was given at least one hour each week to sit and talk with Julie. This was exclusively *my* time to share the joys and frustrations, hopes and struggles related to Bridges, as well as to talk over bread-and-butter working matters. I learnt a great deal from those meetings and discovered what a privilege it was to be offered such quality time.

I believe that Jesus is ready to do the same for us today. He is always willing to meet us at the point of our concerns. But it means struggling past our human instinct to deal with things by ourselves, and taking the time to chat to God. When we do, we will discover that Jesus gently comes alongside us, reminding us of his promises and giving us hope through his unmistakable presence:

> We need to risk that [God] is good by telling our stories. We need to depend on his grace as we face our ugly passions. We need to trust that he will let us find him by entrusting to him the most profound, disappointed passion in our hearts.
>
> *(Larry Crabb)*[4]

Returning to Luke: Jesus' encounter with the woman is a very special one in which he enables a social outcast to have precedence over the waiting Jairus. Perhaps this helps to explain why he felt the incident was incomplete until he had seen, heard and affirmed her. He ends their meeting with one of the wisest and most beautifully constructed sentences I have ever read:

> 'My daughter, your faith has made you well. Go in peace.'
>
> *(Luke 8:48)*

- This is a woman who has felt alienated from society. She was probably wondering whether God accepted or cared for her in her unclean condition. *And Jesus calls her 'daughter'.* A man of proven spiritual authority assures her of her immense value in his eyes. Now she belongs to someone important.

- In desperation, she has reached out to touch Jesus, aware that she is making him unclean, but pinning her hopes on his reputation as a remarkable healer. *Jesus says, 'Your faith has made you well.'* Her actions are vindicated, her uncertainty is given spiritual credibility, and the healing is affirmed as real.

- Finally, Jesus' words, *'Go in peace'*, seep into the heart of a woman for whom there have been twelve years of

physical and social disability, mental anguish and disease.
Now the long wait is ended; her torture is over. There is
no need to be anxious any more. Jesus' actions are sure
and certain.

It is difficult to assess the impact my efforts at listening had on the
lives of the young people I encountered through the lodgings
scheme at Bridges. But if it gave a fraction of the wondrous healing and soothing comfort that the woman received when she met
Jesus, then I can be sure that a very positive connection was made
with a group of vulnerable young people.

## Think about

* Read Luke 24:13–24 (the journey to Emmaus). (You
  might like to use the Bible passage as a starting point for
  prayer or to reflect on the following.)

* In a pressurised situation, Jesus could still allow a
  desperate woman the time and space to talk. He was very
  sensitive to the times when others needed to share with
  him or when he needed to ask a significant question. Both
  situations might lead to a life-changing encounter.

* In the contexts you have chosen to focus on, is there any
  situation in which meaningful conversations can occur?
  Can they be created? Conversations will sometimes be
  private, so be careful to avoid situations that leave you
  open to accusations of abuse. For example, it is wise not
  to meet a young person on their own in a closed room
  away from others. In all situations, there is a need to
  deveop policies on good and safe practice.

* Are you able to listen to others, free of your own
  concerns? Practise concentrating fully on what someone is
  saying to you, even if only for a few minutes at a time. If
  you sense that an important exchange is happening, are
  you flexible enough to allow space for this to develop, or
  to come back to it?

• For those who are individually or corporately aiming to work with people at the edge, does the organisation of your role or project, or the number of helpers, allow for others to have space to tell you some of their story, if they wish to? Are people available to listen? Be aware of the dangers of being just a listener. Do not stop being a real person who also shares.

## Notes

1   Henri Nouwen, *Reaching Out: The three movements of the spiritual life*, Fount, HarperCollins, 1980, p88.

2   Nouwen, *Reaching Out*, p60.

3   Joan Searle, *The Importance of Listening*, Guild of Health, 1984.

4   Lawrence J Crabb, *Moving Through Your Problems Toward Finding God*, Scripture Press, 1994, p198.

*Chapter 5*

# IDENTIFICATION

*It is not the book or the class or the idea that changes us, as important as those things are; it is the experience. Invariably, it's an experience of crossing over boundaries, touching someone else's reality, and hearing other's stories that changes people.*

(Jim Wallis)[1]

I am not sure if anything could have adequately prepared me for my working role at Bridges. However, before telling you more of that journey, I want to describe two significant experiences prior to my time at Bridges, which shaped my thinking and outlook.

The first took place in Canning Town, East London, where, at the age of eighteen, I chose to spend ten days at the Mayflower Family Centre as a member of a Crusader project. It was the distinctive contribution of Pip Wilson, Mayflower's senior youth worker, that was so significant in helping the group both to gel and to explore issues together. When we all returned the following year as an unofficial second Crusader group, the programme included the testimony of Jerry, supervisor of the weights room at the senior youth club. I remember being perched on the back of a red, vandal-proof seating unit in the club coffee-bar, as Jerry began his story. And I vividly recall how shaken I was by something he said.

Jerry had grown up locally, in Canning Town. As a young man he had encountered and occasionally exploited the illegal possibilities that were available. However, in early adulthood he made a decision to follow Jesus (I cannot remember how). It was not an easy choice to make nor was it easy to sustain in the light of the pressures still around him. After a while, in fact, Jerry found himself slipping back into his old ways and receiving goods he knew to be stolen. It was this revelation that startled me.

'Hold on a minute,' I found myself thinking. 'That doesn't make sense. How can you break the law like that and still call yourself a Christian?'

As Jerry continued, I waited for him to acknowledge that this meant he had lost his faith. When this admission did not materialise, I began to struggle to work out why. Evidently Jerry and I had grown up in very different circumstances and, like anyone, we had been influenced by the culture that surrounded us in our formative years. Some of the pressures he had faced were certainly unfamiliar to my experience. What I was beginning to realise, however, was that I had somehow presumed that certain sinful actions were incompatible with the Christian faith and not others. In the light of the environment in which Jerry had led his everyday life, were criminal acts such as receiving stolen goods less acceptable in God's sight than for example, a blinding hatred of another person, which could as easily corrupt the mind of a Christian from the suburbs?

In the months that followed, I began my second year of Sociology Studies at university. As one of five options, I chose Criminology and it was this that introduced me to the challenging ideas on Deviancy contained within Labelling Theory. This theory is concerned with the process by which people come to be labelled as deviant and how others may treat them differently because of this label. It also considers how people come to accept their labels, and the impact this has on them and on their behaviour once they have done so.

> [Deviance is] not a property inherent in certain forms of behaviour; it is a property conferred upon those forms by the audiences which directly or indirectly witness them. Sociologically then, the critical variable is the social audience...
>
> *(K Erikson)*[2]

One of the examples offered by our lecturer, as evidence for the viability of Erikson's supposition, was the following.

A police officer is monitoring traffic by the roadside and sees a vehicle travelling ten miles an hour above the legal speed limit for that road; so the driver is clearly breaking an agreed boundary. Whether his actions are actually prosecuted (labelled deviant), however, depends upon a number of other factors, such as:

- What sort of car is exceeding the speed limit? Is it a sports car, a family saloon or an old wreck? Does it have any incriminating features? Is it known to be stolen?

- What is the driver's attitude when approached? Is he polite, charming and / or attractive? Does he convey remorse, cheekiness or hostility?

- What sort of working day has the police officer had? Has it been largely unsatisfactory and unproductive? Does stopping someone come as a welcome bit of action? Is the police officer under pressure to increase prosecutions? Is there a speed campaign on this particular road?

Labelling, and associated theories concerning deviance, made me think again about my perspectives on life. I found that I was no longer content to accept at face value the labelling of someone as a 'criminal', with all its associated negativity and reinforcement of that person as somehow different from others. To do so before considering other factors seemed simplistic and dismissive.

Bridges brought me face to face with three significant realities. First, ideas which had been formulating as a consequence of the Mayflower project, and thinking that had been challenged through studying theories like Labelling, suddenly started connecting with my life at the project. Second, through being so close to others that my life was very visible, I had to grapple with what being a positive Christian presence really meant. Finally, by living alongside the project users I began to understand much more about them and the direction their lives sometimes took. The day I bought my first ever packet of cigarettes is a case in point.

Angie had come to the centre earlier that day with her two young children, Naomi and James. She was obviously uptight and it was not surprising: two days previously her boyfriend (and the father of James) had left and the children were not responding well to the change. Meanwhile, the neighbours were moaning about Angie's pet greyhound and threatening to complain to the relevant authorities. Julie was so concerned about Angie being close to breaking point, she made a very unusual decision. She informed Angie that she had such fears for the well-being of the children, we were going to look after them at Bridges for a few hours to give Angie space to calm down. Angie exploded with anger. But, as she was restrained, she broke down in the safe and loving arms of the workers with her.[3] A few minutes later I bought the cigarettes, drove Angie and her friend, Theresa, to a home nearby, and then handed over the packet to assist the process of recuperation – I could fully appreciate the need!

My next priority was to make a pot of tea. Sometime later, towards the end of the relaxed conversation that followed, Angie said quietly, 'I'd quite like to be a nun. It would be so peaceful.'

Had my cup not been empty, I would have choked on its contents! But, away from the pressures of everyday life and in the sympathetic presence of others, a young mum recalled something of her Catholic roots and considered for a moment how different life might be in other circumstances. I could perfectly understand how the safety, security and predictability of a convent might seem an attractive alternative to her current life. There were others, well-known to Bridges, for whom an institutional environment seemed to become the safest option. Leonard, sadly, grew accustomed to a prison environment and struggled to make positive use of his free-dom in the outside world. Marjorie, a woman in her late twenties, whose only child had been taken into care a few years previously, spent the majority of her time in the psychiatric units of local hospitals. Here she had some safety from harming herself, as she so often seemed intent on making the ultimate escape from the emotional pain she carried.

These are tragic stories, and I wish they and others had been different. But I can appreciate something of why they were not.

Many of us grow familiar with living in a particular way or with seeing ourselves in a certain light. So when change occurs it feels disconcerting and unsafe, and there may be a strong urge to retreat to the familiar. For those without the confidence gained from discovering that taking risks can be very worthwhile, the pull to go back is very strong. In the case of project users settling into a new home, job or relationship (even one they wanted), the pattern of past failures could be so prevalent in their minds, that future disappointment seemed a certainty. Rather than be hurt again, it was better to press the self-destruct button at an early stage, or at the first sign of what appeared an inevitable outcome.

It was one Friday evening, twenty-one months into my time at Bridges, when the full extent of the change in my understanding came starkly into focus. It was 12 July, and the Bridges team was sighing with relief at the end of another hard week. In fact the recent behaviour of a small group of hostel residents had been so unacceptable that the decision had been taken to ask them to stay elsewhere for two nights, and they were helped to make alternative arrangements. So we finished work in the knowledge that for once none of us were required for hostel duty that night, or as back-up support. In celebration, four of the team decided to go to a nightclub after the usual Friday night visit to the pub. In my role as the alcohol-free driver for the evening, I negotiated the use of my parents' car. It was a great night of fun and we got back to Hatfield at around four in the morning.

On the Sunday, as some hostel residents returned, news began to filter through the grapevine that a group of young people, including residents, had been detained by police somewhere on the south coast. By Monday it had been ascertained that the group had siphoned petrol from a car in Hatfield to provide fuel for their stolen vehicle, just about the time the nightclubbers had returned home. At first I was struck by the coincidental nature of the proximity of the two groups, and wondered what might have occurred had our paths crossed. However, as I thought about the incident, several other features of our respective evenings came to mind. This is how I found myself viewing the two Friday night scenarios:

On Friday 12 July, four people were planning to go out for a drink and then off to a nightclub.

*On Friday 12 July, five people were having a drink in a house, dreaming of a trip down to Brighton.*

Having had a little to drink, the four were fondly anticipating the nightclub trip to come.

*Having had a little to drink, two of the five found themselves increasingly warming to the idea of a trip to Brighton. The group was persuaded to be party to illegal activity.*

The four were able to borrow a car. After a drink with friends, they went off to the club with money to spend.

*The five didn't have access to a vehicle. In fact, for various reasons, none were permitted to drive anyway. However, they did know how to break into cars.*

In the next few hours, the four had a good time at the nightclub and, later, enjoyed a meal at a motorway service station.

*In the next few hours, the five had a good time nicking a car and prepared to go to Brighton.*

At about 4.15 am, the four returned happily to their homes in Hatfield and went to bed content.

*At about 4.15 am, the five stopped off in Hatfield to siphon petrol from another car.*

For the remainder of the weekend, the four went about the rest of their lives a little tired but all the better for the relaxation; they could tell others about the good time they had enjoyed.

*For the remainder of the weekend, the five found themselves in cells being questioned about their activities. They were charged and would appear in court soon. They faced prison, the detention centre, fines or hours of community service, depending on the individual. Most felt bad about their evening's entertainment, and the negative effects would last much longer.*

What do you think about these two stories? Do you find them interesting, remarkable or just curious? What strikes you first – the similarities or the differences between the two sets of events?

At the time, and it remains the case today, it is the similarities that I see most prominently. This is because so much of what the other group did resonated with my own aspirations and actions that evening.

- Both groups wanted to go out somewhere different.

- Both were keen to make the most of a change in the usual routine in order to have a good time.

- The camaraderie, conversation and excitement all led to unusual ideas and actions.

- They both needed a vehicle to accomplish what they wanted to do.

- They were enjoying the freedom of being able to choose where to go and what to do.

The group of five were not anonymous but real people whom I knew, individually and personally. As Jim Wallis suggests in the quote at the beginning of the chapter, if we spend time alongside those who have a life experience and a view of life that is different from our own, and we are willing to engage with this difference, then we are likely to change. I know that I did.

Three things will make a significant difference to our perspective.

- Where we stand in relation to life
- Who we listen to in life
- The presence of meaningful relationships

In the Gospels, we see Jesus identifying with those at the edge in such a way that the poor, neglected and marginalised felt loved and understood. Luke 7:36–50 presents an opportunity to witness an intriguing encounter that takes this theme further. (You may like to read the passage at this point.)

> A Pharisee invited Jesus to have dinner with him, and
> Jesus went to his house and sat down to eat. In that town
> was a woman who lived a sinful life. She heard that Jesus
> was eating in the Pharisee's house, so she brought an
> alabaster jar full of perfume and stood behind Jesus, by his
> feet, crying and wetting his feet with her tears.
>
> *(Luke 7:36–38)*

The Pharisees were an exclusive group (their name in Hebrew means 'separatist') who adhered very closely to God's laws, particularly in the areas of tithing, Sabbath observance and meals. Ritual purity at mealtimes, including the correct preparation of food, was very important. Indeed, the Pharisees were known as a table-fellowship who were very restrictive about the company they kept on such occasions. They drew a sharp line between those who kept the law and those who did not; those who did not were 'sinners' with whom they would not eat. So this was no casual invitation to dinner that Jesus had accepted: to be invited was a mark of respect, and Jesus was fully aware of the religious and cultural implications.

The woman is unnamed but not unknown. To those around the table, she was a sinner with a reputation; she was very much uninvited, unwanted, unwelcome. Aware of this, she bravely entered and attached herself to Jesus on whom her intended actions were focused. We can easily appreciate why the woman's appearance was so offensive to this exclusive gathering. Naturally, the host, Simon, reacted to her presence:

> When the Pharisee saw this, he said to himself, 'If this
> man really were a prophet, he would know who this
> woman is who is touching him; he would know what kind
> of sinful life she lives!'
>
> *(Luke 7:39)*

That Jesus allowed this woman to continue to make her offering was, for Simon, a reason to doubt the authenticity of his spiritual status. Jesus, of course, knew who the woman was and what her life up till then had been like. He recognised, more than any of them, the implications of her intrusion and the meaning of her actions. Table-fellowship was also very important for Jesus, but his view on who he shared meals with was vastly different from the Pharisees and presented Simon with a challenge.

> Jesus' eating habits radically threatened the social–
> religious world of his opponents. For Jesus to share a table
> with outcasts, thereby suggesting their acceptance by God,
> was to threaten the central ordering principle of the Jewish
> social world: the division between purity and impurity,
> holy and not holy, righteous and wicked.
>
> *(Simon Steer)*[4]

Jesus also knew and loved Simon. He responded directly to Simon's doubts by telling a brief but powerful story:

> 'There were two men who owed money to a
> moneylender,' Jesus began. 'One owed him five hundred
> silver coins, and the other owed him fifty. Neither of them
> could pay him back, so he cancelled the debts of both.
> Which one, then, will love him more?'
>
> *(Luke 7:41–42)*

By inviting Jesus to a meal, Simon has placed himself and Jesus in the same group – among the pure and holy, the fellowship of non-sinners. Conversely, the woman is an outsider and one of the sinners. But, as the story unfolds, it is clear that Jesus is implying that *he* is the moneylender, that Simon is the character who owes fifty coins, and the woman the one who owes five hundred. Jesus is purposefully moving Simon into a different position. Like the woman, he is in debt to the moneylender, he is powerless to pay it back, and he is entirely reliant on the grace of the moneylender to release him from the debt. What Simon and this woman have in common far outweighs the scale of the debt, which is the only factor that separates them. The radical shift Jesus makes to Simon's position is a challenge to all of us for any time when, as

Christians, we use the label 'non-Christian' in a way that holds us apart from others, or subtly creates an attitude of superiority which can easily filter through into our behaviour towards others. In fact the reality of my Bridges experience was that, as time went on, I identified more with project users. Furthermore, by journeying alongside people like Angie, the more I discovered what we had in common.

> Getting close enough to see, hear, touch, smell and taste
> the reality of others is what always makes the difference.
> In listening to the stories of those so seemingly different
> from us, we find similar but unexpressed voices inside of
> ourselves ... the beginning of new understanding and the
> foundation of compassionate action.
>
> *(Jim Wallis)*[5]

As I began genuinely to empathise, I believe I caught a glimpse of the compassionate understanding Jesus had. His capacity to empathise with others made him effective in serving their needs.

The wonder of Jesus is that if anyone had the right to set himself apart, it was he. Instead, the unrighteous, the condemned and the spiritually abandoned felt able to approach him and were welcomed when they did so. The woman in the Gospel story was probably a known prostitute. She invaded an exclusive meal amongst religious men. She untied her hair, which was considered shameful in the presence of men, and used it to wipe Jesus' feet. In effect, one of the tools of her notorious trade features in an act of worship. Jesus not only accepted this offering, he held the woman up as an example of love to those who believed themselves to have nothing in common with her. For Simon the Pharisee, the woman had disrupted and brought shame to a significant social gathering. But Jesus acknowledged her welcome and the extravagance of the care and attention she lavishes on him. He saw it as a sign of transformation that was going on deep within her heart.

Kathy Galloway imagines what might have been said had there been a fuller version of Jesus' words to Simon:

> She's done a lot of things in her life that she's ashamed of
> ... she's known the wretchedness and loneliness of hating
> herself ... but she can still find it within herself to do
> something of beauty and selflessness ... you don't know
> how good life feels when it's given back to you ... There
> are deep wounds of pain and suffering within her that
> every passing encounter drove deeper. But take the guilt
> and shame away and the great holes can become filled
> with love, deep springs welling up and overflowing.[6]

Jesus' ability to empathise with others (especially those at the edge) helped him to perceive and interpret the profoundly spiritual nature of their heartfelt responses. This led him to make public statements like 'Your sins are forgiven' (Luke 7:48), which caused consternation because they broke apart existing religious assumptions about who possessed spiritual insight, whose heart was right before God and which person could be a follower of Jesus. Of course, it also revealed Jesus' perception about his identity, which many religious people could not accept.

When seeking to make connections with those who are outside the church or who have no experience of the Christian faith, Christians often demand that they grasp something of theology or an understanding of faith before making a personal response. Today, as fewer people have knowledge of the gospel, its credibility is, apparently, diminishing; perhaps Christians should instead be striving to introduce people to a faith that invites them into the loving presence of Jesus. Then later, once they have made a personal response to him, their actions can be affirmed and the significance explained.

Jesus fully identified with people; he was on their level and he understood them. He also fully identified with his Father, so that he never compromised on standards. As people experienced his humanity, they also began to glimpse his deity. As he confronted them on a human level, his godly loving kindness came shining through. At Bridges, I found that the more time I spent alongside project users, and the more I was committed to their welfare, the more I was able to identify with them and, consequently, to connect with them. The challenge for Christians is not only to be committed enough to others to do this, but still to remain different; to identify with others but also to be identified by them as God's people; to be holy but not 'holier than thou'.

> That is holiness. It never abandons, it identifies deeply with individual people. But it also bring the reality of God's presence, the purity of his holiness.
>
> *(Rebecca Pippert)*[7]

## Think about

*   Read Luke 14:15–24; 18:9–14; Mark 10:17,20–23. (You might like to use the Bible passages as a starting point for prayer or to reflect on the following.)

*   Jesus' ability to identify with the woman meant that he could understand her actions and accept her response to him.

*   Look again at the incidents of 12 July described in the chapter, and answer the questions posed there. Reflect carefully on the possible reasons for your response, such as the influences that shape your perspective on life.

*   Identify one or two people within the context on which you have chosen to focus, or within the work you are doing with people at the edge. Aim to get to know them, particularly by seeking to accept and understand them in a loving way. Be interested but not intrusive, and prepared to share significant moments of your own story.

*   The woman used an expensive perfume, among other things, in her response to Jesus. What might you use and how would you use it? What about the people you have just identified? How might they respond, and what would they use?

# Notes

1    Jim Wallis, *The Soul of Politics*, HarperCollins, 1995, p178.

2    K Erikson, 'Notes on the sociology of deviance', *The Other Side: Perspectives on Deviance*, H S Becker (ed), Free Press United States.

3    It is important to understand that Julie had known Angie since her teenage years (that is, for at least seven years) when this all took place.

4    Simon Steer, from a lecture at the Institute for Contemporary Christianity, 1997.

5    Wallis, *Politics*, p176.

6    Kathy Galloway, *Imagining the Gospels*, SPCK, 1994, p92.

7    Pippert, *Saltshaker*, p90.

*Chapter 6*

# READINESS

*A place where the system is most open to
change is what I call a 'free space'; a time
when the system is most open to change is
what I call a 'fluid phase'. In my experience
'free spaces' and 'fluid phases' are not so
much to be defined as to be discerned. We can
sense the 'free spaces' and 'fluid phases'
which can present us with a chance to act
creatively for change.*

(Dave Andrews)[1]

When a small dog peed down my ankle, it brought a whole new
meaning to the phrase 'You've got legs like tree-trunks'. It also
took me greatly by surprise. The setting of the Buddhist temple,
'Swaymbhunath' in Kathmandu, was a most unlikely venue for
such an attack, and his moment of relief – as I was taking a pho-
tograph of a holy man decked out in flowing orange robes – was
cleverly chosen. The fact that I was wearing shorts at the time
made the whole experience unforgettable.

What I also remember about that day were the beggars who lined
the steps on the approach to the temple. Each one seemed to have
their appointed spot along the path. Some had arms outstretched,
others kept their bodies bowed. One or two spoke, most were silent.
There were those with obvious physical disabilities, while others
were probably the casualties of life or the social system. I sensed that
many had been there for some time, and wondered what it would be
like to be sitting in the same place, day after day, hoping to stir the
consciences of people going to and fro from the temple; to be so
entirely dependent on the goodwill of others.

This was the everyday reality for the person at the heart of the Gospel story we are about to consider. His problems were compounded by the fact that he was also blind. (You may want to read the story in Luke 18:35–43 or to keep it open for reference.) We meet Bartimaeus[2] sitting at the roadside near Jericho. He was wondering why so many people were rushing by. When he discovered that Jesus was the cause, he called out to him. I wonder if this was typical of Bartimaeus – whether he was known locally as 'that noisy beggar', or did he make a louder noise that day? What is certain is that he irritated the surrounding crowd: 'The people in front scolded him and told him to be quiet' (Luke 18:39).

However Bartimaeus was a determined character and, after his repeated cries, Jesus responded. Why? What was it that made Jesus pause, in the midst of a pressing crowd, to meet a blind beggar?

•   Was he simply responding to a plea for help?

•   Was it that Jesus heard Bartimaeus call out more than once and took this as a sign of real need?

•   Was there something about the beggar's tone of voice?

•   Was it because Bartimaeus referred to Jesus' royal lineage, from whom the Messiah was promised to come, and linked this to his own need for help?

•   Was Jesus simply led by the prompting of the Holy Spirit?

It could have been one or a combination of these alternatives that explains Jesus' response. Whatever his reasons, Jesus sensed that Bartimaeus was ready to meet him and this was the right moment to stop.

At the beginning of this chapter, Dave Andrews describes two types of occasion within social organisations and systems when there is increased potential for change. He calls the *place* where this is possible a 'free space', and for the *time* of opportunity he uses the expression 'a fluid phase.' But there are places and times in the lives of *people* which are more conducive to change.

Retreat houses and holiday homes, where one can 'get away from it all', are examples of places where a person might consider change. Sometimes we stumble across these places unexpectedly, for example during a thought-provoking conversation, from a chance meeting with a stranger, or from an inspirational book. The same is true of time. Many people turn to counsellors or others for advice in a crisis or at other significant periods in their lives. This might happen when they reach a milestone in life, such as parenthood or retirement, or another potential trigger for change.

I want to tell you about three conversations that took place at Bridges when three young men reached a free space or fluid phase within their lives and it was my privilege to be present.

## Dane

Dane first came to Bridges soon after I began there. He was fifteen and living with his parents just a mile from the project. But conflict at home was making life difficult, especially between Dane and his father. In the months leading up to Dane's move into the hostel, he appeared at the centre a few times, sometimes in a crisis. On one occasion, his friends came to Bridges for help because Dane was sitting alongside a nearby railway bridge, glue-sniffing and hitting himself over the head with a milk bottle. Dane was intelligent, sensitive and articulate, but he could also slip into very dark moods.

By the age of nineteen he had left the hostel, spent time in different local lodgings and then moved into more independent accommodation. The glue-sniffing phase had passed but resurfaced as drug use, and, as the frequency of Dane's visits to the project fell significantly, there was concern that his drug use had become dependence. Then one day Dane wandered into Bridges. Within a few moments of arriving he was asking me if he could see Julie, the project coordinator – but she was talking privately to someone else. There was something about Dane's manner which suggested that this was no casual request, so I offered him the opportunity to talk to me. To my surprise he accepted. In the quiet of Bridges 'graffiti room' Dane came quickly to the point.

He realised he had a drug problem and he wanted to do something about it. I knew enough to realise that this moment of self-realisation and resolve needed to be exploited. Within minutes Julie's conversation had been interrupted, within hours she had obtained a place at a rehabilitation centre, and, by the end of the day, Dane had arrived there.

## Gerry

On a Monday, when the drop-in centre was at its busiest, I greeted Gerry at the top of the stairs. It was an unlikely place to begin a conversation of any importance, as we were on the landing near the toilet and at a thoroughfare between three upstairs rooms. Somehow, though, a fleeting word developed into a longer verbal exchange.

Gerry was a twenty-one-year-old Scot who had moved down from his native country four years previously in order to be near relatives. He soon became one of Bridges' most frequent and well-known visitors. During this time he established a significant relationship with another regular project user named Denise. Both were charming, quick-witted, fiercely determined and often fiery. It required courage to be in the vicinity during one of their heated arguments. Gerry and Denise went on to have a beautiful daughter called Marsha, who had inherited her parents' strength of personality and sparkle around the eyes. The Bridges team wondered how Gerry's patience would cope with the persistent demands of a young child. There were concerns for Denise too, as a teenage parent, but she had wanted a baby for some time and seemed better prepared for this than Gerry.

At the top of the stairs, visitors to the centre were still walking between us, but Gerry did not use this distraction as an opportunity to end our conversation. I had unwittingly stumbled across a time when Gerry was feeling thoughtful. I probed a little more than usual and responded to his willingness to share by disclosing some of my own story. Most of all I listened. The topic worked its way round to fatherhood, and Gerry told me about an occasion when Marsha seemed to be choking on some food. It was clear to see how a worried young parent might strike the back of a child with an excessive force in a moment of acute anxiety. I took the opportunity to express that I understood how this might easily happen; in doing so I was giving Gerry a chance to admit that he had lost control in a moment of panic or had hit Marsha inappropriately on other occasions after losing his patience. I was somewhat reassured when an admission failed to materialise and a significant conversation continued.

## Callum

A shared love of football was the initial reason why Callum and I got on well together. As an avid Arsenal fan, it was not long before glorious praise of 'The Gunners' was appearing in our graffiti room and elsewhere. Callum was generally good company – bubbly, cheeky, fast-talking and with a winning smile. He was also capable of maintaining employment; a characteristic that provided him with a good choice of lodgings when he left Bridges. After that he visited the centre much less often, but Callum kept in touch with me by periodically visiting me at home. This was something few project users ever did, but Callum never abused the privilege.

Callum's verbal output maintained its high frequency even when his mood dipped, and his contribution became very negative during those times. During the latter years of my project work, Bridges took on a closely supportive role with a nearby hostel called Mimram, and Callum had a spell living there when his accommodation fell through following the loss of his job. He was having a bad spell, losing his car and experiencing conflict with girlfriend Jo.

One sunny day, while visiting the Mimram office, I noticed Callum and Jo arguing outside. She was trying to walk away, but he was insisting that, before she went, she should return a ring he had given her. Eventually he came back alone and I went to find him. We had talked many times in the four years I had known him, but on this occasion I decided to interject after only a few minutes of listening so that I could share an interpretation of his situation which I felt might be helpful. I told Callum that it seemed to me that his heart was like a bottle half full of a liquid containing the murky elements of possessiveness and dislike of himself. On the surface of the liquid, like a skin, were his job, car and girlfriend. Recently Callum had lost the first two and now he was facing major problems with Jo. This meant that the skin was broken, and the murky elements that had been churned up were floating to the surface. Just as I was wondering how Callum would react to this picture, he broke down. Through painful tears he said, 'Something inside me makes me do it ... I'm nothing ... I have some growing up to do.' For the first and only time, I took a specific illustration from a Christian book and applied it directly to someone from Bridges. After a four-year relationship, during which I had got to know Callum well, it was worth taking the risk to see whether or not my hunch was inspired.

None of these three stories should be considered without the recognition that they occurred three to four years after I had met the young men concerned; after countless hours spent laughing, cajoling, sympathising, breaking up fights, going on rides at Alton Towers and drinking hundreds of mugs of tea and coffee with them. It was our shared history that prepared the ground and enabled me to sense when they were in a free space or a fluid phase. If an opportunity like this can be seized sensitively, the result is a greater depth of relationship and the satisfaction of assisting someone else to move forward in their personal development and awareness.

Julie had a great ability to make these sorts of connections. I want to outline four elements based on her skills and experience, which may improve our ability to do the same.

## Spotting opportunities

A typical working day at Bridges included a significant amount of time in the company of project users. However, remaining alert to opportunities for a significant exchange within that time – and, in Julie's case, being able to subtly manufacture them – required skill and experience. Often Julie was up-front in creating space to chat with someone, and usually her boldness carried it off. As a community-based worker who travelled round the local area, one of my most frequently used means of chatting was the car. Asking for company on a journey was one straightforward way to create a non-threatening environment in which to talk to someone who seemed fed up or with whom I needed to explore a general concern.

## Fishing bravely

Being able to spot a suitable opportunity is very different from using it effectively. Julie's warm and winning manner, allied with her obvious commitment to the well-being of project users, enabled her to do both successfully. Where conversations touched on delicate or difficult concerns, being willing to broach the topic required real courage. My talk on the stairs with Gerry included a technique that Julie described to the team as 'fishing'. This involved dropping a remark into a conversation like an angler uses bait. If the other person seemed interested or took it up, the topic was continued. If the bait was ignored or rejected, this was also noted and the conversation moved on to something else. But the potential was there for the topic to be raised again later.

## Consciously shelving

One particular phrase of Julie's, which caused the most hilarity among the team and which will forever be associated with her, was 'shelves in the mind'. It was her way of describing the process that happened after noticing something said or done by a project user. Instead of giving an instant response, the hearer stored the words or actions on 'shelves in the mind' – logged them away, if you like, until an appropriate moment. When that moment arrived, the shelves were raided and the person who had been guarding the information might say, 'Do you remember doing that?' or 'Are you the same person I heard saying that?'

## Checking out

One of the greatest strengths of Bridges' working practice was its teamwork. This was sustained through meetings, regular recordings made on the progress of individual project users, and the latest news shared via the communication book. Through access to these, workers were always aware of the current situation.

Meetings provided regular forums in which to discuss issues and concerns where workers had the opportunity to check with colleagues any important news, gossip or suspicion that they had about life at the project. Sometimes this led to an agreed course of action, with one key person designated to carry it out. However, by being part of the decision-making process we could all be consistent in our approach and supportive to the team member most involved.

I believe that the skill and sensitivity of Julie's approach had a Christlike flavour to it. For those committed to mission at the edge, emulating these principles will help to deepen relationships and enable people to make progress. In addition, they provide helpful pointers for introducing others to Jesus.

- Christians need to be alert for the spaces that enable significant encounters, or for the times when another person is in a particularly reflective or open frame of mind.

- Showing commitment to others means watching and listening to them lovingly and carefully, helpfully reminding them of things past when they need hope, encouragement or a personal challenge.

- When Jesus called his disciples, he said, 'From now on you will be catching people' (Luke 5:10). Sometimes Christians will need to 'fish' in order to gauge interest or to discover if they have found an opportune moment in which to talk about Jesus and their relationship with him. Julie often used the phrase 'caring enough to confront'. The word 'confront' means to 'bring into the presence of'. Christians must be ready and willing to make others aware of Jesus' presence.

- For those building relationships at the edge, the partnership of others is important. The prayerful house group, or support group, can be both an inspiration and a

wise back-up in terms of faith-sharing. In addition, I
believe that those who are supported in prayer will find
renewed strength and a greater sensitivity to times of
opportunity. Jesus provides the model: so in touch with his
Father that he has a clear purpose; so rooted in a loving
relationship with him that he is not self-conscious. These
two qualities enhance his commitment to others and his
capacity to be truly altruistic.

While I was at Bridges, I never quite managed to become a consistently skilful practitioner at being ready, willing and able to
seize the moment. One of my struggles centred round the occasions when my readiness and my ability to confront were clouded
by irritation or a personal agenda. In these situations, I placed so
much emphasis on confronting someone's behaviour or resolving
a particular issue that my capacity to spot, 'fish', observe or check
out, was hindered or skewed. I had 'got locked into a personal
mission' (Julie's description for this attitude). I sometimes fell
into doing this in my relationship with Denise, Gerry's partner,
and it affected my ability to build a consistently effective relationship with her. Jesus was locked into a heavenly mission in the
sense that he wanted others to discover who he was and to know
that, through him, they could be put right with God. However, he
never allowed irritation to cloud his judgement, or neglected people's feelings in the face of his pressing spiritual agenda.

One of the other potential pitfalls of being 'locked into a personal mission' is that the lead comes from the one who decides
that they must confront, irrespective of whether the other person
is ready. This is not a feature of Jesus' encounter with
Bartimaeus. First, Jesus responds to Bartimaeus' cry for help.
Then, when they come face to face, he asks a remarkable question, which hands the initiative back to the blind beggar: 'What do
you want me to do for you?' (Luke 18:41).

Everyone knew that Bartimaeus was blind, so it seems a foolish question – until, that is, you begin to appreciate that a blind
beggar has many needs – for shade, for friendship and for financial security. Jesus opens a door of opportunity for Bartimaeus;

but, if he is to be transformed, he has to want the very best for himself and to trust Jesus enough to ask for it – and he does. Bartimaeus asks for his eyes to be opened so that he can see the world around him. However, when they are opened, he receives a second sight: he is confronted with the wonder of God's love and compassion. Jesus is standing before him:

> At once, he was able to see, and he followed Jesus, giving thanks to God.
>
> *(Luke 18:43)*

As with so many of his personal encounters, Jesus' response not only met the immediate wishes of Bartimaeus, they also helped him to discover a new and unforeseen dimension.

Jesus was always ready to confront others and help them make fresh discoveries about life, themselves and God. He was the catalyst for the Danes, Gerrys and Callums of his day to make connections that were life-changing. Let us pray that God will help us be loving, wise, courageous, alert and sensitive to the free spaces and fluid phases in others' lives, as we seek to follow Jesus' example in making connections with them.

## Think about

* Read 2 Corinthians 1:3–4; 1 Peter 3:15. (You might like to use the Bible passages as a starting point for prayer or to reflect on the following.)

* Jesus knew that it was the right moment to stop and for Bartimaeus to meet him. This led to a life-changing encounter for Bartimaeus.

* Getting to know others and building up trust takes time. Be aware that for people at the edge it may take longer. Try to use your knowledge of others positively in order to develop a deeper link. For example, notice when they are preoccupied and give them space; make the most of times when the general mood is reflective; show sensitivity when they are facing tough situations.

- Sometimes relationships do not deepen naturally over time, as you hoped. Are you prepared to take the initiative, or the risk, to see if there is a positive response?

- Are you willing to share your Christian faith, to talk honestly about how it began and the comfort and hope that it brings.

- If you are seeking to deepen a friendship or to introduce someone to Jesus, but are being frustrated, remember that we can only provide opportunities. The issue cannot be forced.

## Notes

1   Andrews, *A Better World*, p150.

2   Not all scholars agree that the blind beggar in Luke is the same as the Bartimaeus named in Mark 10:46–52. However, we will continue to refer to him here as Bartimaeus.

*Chapter 7*

# LINKING

**link** v. *to join or connect, to unite, to be connected.*

(The University English Dictionary)

Have you ever sat on the concrete pavement of a busy street, at a different level to the many people walking by? I have done so a few times in and around the Strand in Central London. From this position, the passing world is dominated by legs, knees and ankles, skirts, jeans and suit trousers, or trainers, heels and shiny black shoes. (Offering sandwiches and chatting to homeless people is one of the many activities of City Connections, a project organised by myself for Frontier Youth Trust and Crusaders; it is the successor to the Mayflower work party mentioned at the start of chapter five.)

One of my strongest memories is of sitting down opposite a cafe on a Covent Garden street, talking to Russell and Pete. They were delighted with the offer of ham sandwiches, disappointed that there was no tea, but friendly enough to allow Linda and I to sit and chat with them. Pete bristled when he heard mention of our Christian motivation for being there. He openly shared his anger about the physical punishment administered by his strict, religious father. There was nothing to be said in defence, so we expressed our sadness and gently encouraged him not to write off Jesus completely. Russell was initially reticent, but as the conversation progressed he became the focus of attention. He showed us a philosophy book, one of many he had read, and it was clear that here was a man who thought deeply about life and was asking significant questions. Once, Russell told us, he had challenged God to make himself known. Two days later, while he was lying down in the room where he was living at the time, Russell's rest was disturbed by the presence of a bright light. He visited a clergyman to tell him what had happened, but seemed to have received no encouragement to have faith in what he suspected, and which Linda and I believed was God's reply to his prayer.

I walked away from this encounter with very mixed feelings. It had been a privilege to sit alongside Russell and Pete, and to have them share something of themselves with us. On the other hand, Pete had been damaged by someone who professed to have faith in God; and Russell had experienced God but had no easy access to a situation in which this could be affirmed and pursued. It was sad, but should we have said more? Would it have been right to have offered Russell a way into a friendship with Jesus, then and there? What do you think?

If we had encouraged Russell to ask Jesus to be his friend and Saviour, but had then left him in a social vacuum with no tangible support or fellowship to reinforce the loving message, how would he have felt? I suspect that disappointment would have led to long-term disillusionment.

Providing sandwiches for homeless people is of practical help. Spending time chatting with them says, 'I want to spend time with you, and I am interested in what you have to say.' Having company breaks up the monotony of a long evening. However, it is all too easy to make assumptions about the needs of homeless people; in reality their lives are individual and complex. At Bridges, I worked with people whose early lives were often hallmarked by fractured homes, family conflicts and irreconcilable relational breakdown. Frequently, new residents came to the centre having spent years in different parts of the care system, moving between various hostels, living on friends' floors or in other temporary lodgings. It is easy to appreciate why they took time to feel at home at Bridges. For those who have lived on the streets, who feel looked down on, left out and pushed aside by society at large, the damage must be even greater. So, while it is true that those living at the edge need Jesus, to act on that knowledge with no thought for the wider implications should they choose to accept him, is naive and takes no account of the complexity of the discipling process on the Christian journey.

Jesus went out of his way to meet the Petes and Russells of his day. As Donald Kraybill observes, Jesus 'touched the untouchables, loved the unlovables, and accepted the stigmatized'.[1]

Had Russell sought out Jesus with the determined curiosity he displayed in his reading, he would have been assured of finding complete acceptance. Similarly, Jesus could have healed the hurt that Pete had carried inside him since the abusive treatment from his father. It would certainly have been a life-changing encounter for them both. But how would Jesus have dealt with the wider considerations? Let us take another look at three of the Gospel stories featured so far.

## Shalom

In Luke 8:40–48, when he meets the woman who suffered from persistent bleeding, Jesus ends the encounter with the words, 'Go in peace.' 'Peace' is translated from the Hebrew word *shalom* which has a richer significance than the English word. *Shalom* is derived from a verb that means 'to make complete'; it implies a totality of well-being, a condition when things are as they are meant to be; something, for example, that the woman did not possess in her suffering.

However, *shalom* extends beyond personal wholeness. Rather, it involves 'Health of body, health of mind, health of heart and a whole healthy relationship between human beings and God ... wholeness within a society where each person ... belongs and counts and is valued'.[2] In the story of the woman, therefore, there could be no *shalom* in the society or the religion where she was condemned and excluded. Her healing was a sign of God's kingdom coming into the world. In using the word *shalom* Jesus was affirming its wider significance.

## Status

In Luke 18:35–43, it is the crowd who are keenest to see Jesus tell Bartimaeus to stop shouting. What right has a blind beggar to call out to a great teacher, let alone meet him? But Jesus, having heard his cry, deliberately asks the crowd to bring the beggar to the fore, like courtiers summoning an important guest to the king. Jesus is asking them to grant Bartimaeus the same level of respect in which he holds him. By the end of the encounter, the person they were ignoring is the means by which everyone is praising God. By sharing in the beggar's healing, both he and they are transformed. The crowd moves on and Bartimaeus is lost among Jesus' followers – though an onlooker might have heard him shouting his praises!

## Reintegration

In Luke 8:26–39, after he has been freed from his demons, the man begs Jesus to let him accompany him. But Jesus replies, 'Go back home and tell what God has done for you.' I do not believe that the potential impact of the man's story was Jesus' only consideration in making this response. For a significant time this man had been living at the edge of his society, an alienated figure who often escaped to hide in caves. By giving him an important task to fulfil, Jesus is also providing the means by which he can be reintegrated into his local community, and an opportunity for him to repair damaged relationships.

Jesus had a keen appreciation of the wider context, of the issues and needs surrounding the people he encountered:

> Forgiving sins, welcoming social outcasts like lepers and fallen women into community, miraculously healing the blind and lame . . . Jesus brought a comprehensive healing to the body and soul, individual and community.
>
> *(Ron Sider)*[3]

Within the action of Gospel stories like these, Jesus had two important roles. First, he demonstrated how people on the margins of society should be treated. Second, and central to the theme of this chapter, he acted as a link between the woman, Bartimaeus and the demoniac, and their respective communities. He gave them a way back to others as well as to himself.

Acting as a link, a connecting point, a bridge, was one of our key roles at Bridges (one good reason for its name!). Here are three brief examples of how we fulfilled this role.

# June

She was very much as her name suggests – relaxed and warm, as gentle as a summer's day. But June never hesitated to sit in the noisy mêlée of the main room, quietly chatting to those she knew. June was a health visitor who came to Bridges mainly to see parents with young children, who might not otherwise make it to the health centre. Potential reasons for this included difficulties with transport, anxieties about children, and fears of negative feedback on their parenting ability and of 'interfering' professionals. Encouraging project users to talk regularly to June in the familiar surroundings of Bridges was of immediate practical help, but it was also hoped that it would give them independence: as they came to value her good advice, they would eventually turn more readily to June or other health visitors and away from Bridges. The project was bridging the gap.

# Shirley

By the time I arrived to work at Bridges, the project had already developed a link with the local parish church of St Michael's. Gordon, the vicar, was well-known to the local community, his face beaming at everyone and his cassock billowing wildly as he cycled around the parish. He was one of Bridges' trustees, and the team liked and respected him. I attended St Michael's and contributed articles for the magazine about different aspects of Bridges' work. This is how Shirley came to volunteer, in response to my request for help in the crèche. She helped at one session a week for about a year. I only realised the impact this had made on her when a copy of the letter she had written to the then prime minister appeared in the parish magazine. Through helping at the crèche, Shirley had witnessed the tender and compassionate way in which young men from the project played their part as helpers or parents. This changed her impression of them completely. So when she became aware of proposed homelessness legislation that would penalise those in a similar situation, she felt compelled to write. Shirley had literally been moved to tears.

Wherever possible, the project facilitated links like these

between project users and the community. We believed it was a gradual process of mutual education.

## Mediation

Project workers had an important role to play in being the bridge between two parties who would otherwise have found it hard to relate to each other. This could mean acting as mediator between two hostel residents who were at odds or, as was often my role, sitting alongside someone facing a difficult conversation with another agency. A typical example was an occasion when I accompanied Angie to the local housing office. Due to an accumulation of rent arrears, she was being threatened with eviction from her council house. In the subsequent meeting of the two parties, which I initiated, I tried not to intervene unless clarification was needed or Angie was struggling to explain her situation without getting angry or upset. This role of mediation became increasingly common as I developed more welfare benefits work within Bridges, and its effectiveness depended on two things. First, I had to establish trust with each of the other two parties. Only with this in place could they possibly be enabled to communicate together. I also tried to help both sides understand the needs of the other: in this case, Angie's need to retain as much as possible of her limited income, for her family's sake, and the council's need to see the level of rent arrears consistently coming down.

Since I began working for Frontier Youth Trust, I have been supporting, networking and training Christian youth workers, both voluntary and paid, who are on the frontiers of Christian mission in this country. Using venues like youth clubs, drop-in centres, buses and caravans, they are getting alongside young people and seeking to express God's love to them in ways they can understand. These youth workers have a key role in being a connection to Jesus, standing in the gap between those at the edge and the Christian faith.

Working in this context is challenging, and youth workers may sometimes question whether their work is having any impact.

However, almost all effective youth work is long-term, and when the encouragements come (as they will) it is crucial for them to be noted, discussed and retained as a reminder that God's Holy Spirit is at work. Let me give an example of a conversation I once had at Bridges, which was of great encouragement in this way.

Andy was a long-term hostel resident for whom Bridges managed to arrange an interview with an agency who placed full-time volunteers. One evening Andy and I were chatting about how the interview had gone, and he told me that one of the questions he had been asked concerned how he might get on if the placement was in a Christian project. He went on, 'I said, "Well, there's a Christian where I live now and we seem to get on all right." ' So often, the role of the Christian worker is simply to be a positive influence, breaking down any negative presuppositions someone may have about the Christian faith or being a positive link in the chain. It is my hope that when Andy meets another Christian, he will be more amenable to building a relationship with him or her and, consequently, he will be more open to Jesus.

Garth Hewitt tells the story of a Christian who spent many hours sitting with a chronically depressed man who came from a Hindu background.[4] Eventually the man began to share his burdens. After listening carefully, the Christian said that he felt this man needed God.

'What God?' the man replied. So his new friend talked about Jesus.

'But what's he like?' the man asked.

After some hesitation, the Christian turned to the only common reference point they had. 'Well … he's like me.'

'OK, I'll follow him,' said the man, 'because you have cared for me and listened to me.'

Garth Hewitt goes on to say, 'What an honour it is to be commissioned to be Jesus in a situation!' He ends this story with a prayer by John Henry Newman:

Help me to spread your fragrance everywhere I go. Let me preach you without preaching – not by words but by my example. By the catching force, the sympathetic influence

of what I do, the evident fullness of the love my heart
bears to you.

In the light of Jesus' example, Christians should aspire to be the
means by which the forgotten, left behind and pushed aside are
accepted, valued and reintegrated. In addition, those working with
people at the edge can become a significant person of faith, a connecting point to Jesus, a window through which God is glimpsed.

I will close this chapter by returning to the streets of Covent
Garden with Russell and Pete, where Linda and I offered an
opportunity for some honest sharing about spirituality, faith and
Jesus. However, if Jesus had encountered Russell and Pete, I think
it might have gone like this.

Jesus was on his way to the Covent Garden Opera House,
where a bishop had fallen dangerously ill during the
interval of a performance of *Aida*. Although accompanied
by a large crowd, Jesus noticed Russell sitting with a
friend at the side of the road. He stopped so that he could
meet him. Jesus asked a few of those in the crowd, many
of whom were wearing evening dress, to bring the grubby
Russell to him. He listened as Russell shared his life story.
Despite the fact that nearby restaurant owners had long
resented Russell and his friends as an unwelcome sight in
front of their establishments, Jesus asked them to bring
him some water. 'At last,' some of the crowd thought.
'This homeless man is going to have a good wash!'
However, Jesus baptised Russell and welcomed him as
one of God's people. Russell stood up, beaming, full of
thanks. He hugged Jesus. Some of the crowd cheered,
some wept, some walked off in disgust. And some of the
more religious onlookers wondered if Russell had been on
a discipling course.

Russell wanted to follow Jesus. Would Jesus welcome
him along? Or would he encourage him to travel along the
Strand and to Waterloo Station, sharing what had
happened to him?

# Think about

• Read Matthew 5:13–16; 2 Corinthians 2:14–16; 3:4–6.
(You might like to use the Bible passages as a starting
point for prayer or to reflect on the following.)

• If you have never talked to a beggar sitting on the
pavement, why not do so some time soon? If you pass
someone regularly, get into the habit of chatting.

• Jesus not only spent significant time meeting those at the
edge; but, where possible, he enabled them to be
reconnected to their communities and to other people.

• Realise that you can be a connector, someone with the
potential to use your influence positively. As you develop
relationships in your chosen context or through a specific
project, be aware of the wider needs of those you are
getting to know. For example, can you help to build
bridges between disgruntled neighbours; introduce a new
or shy person into a group of friends at church; or put a
different view to mates at college who are targeting
someone weak?

• You too are the means by which others catch a glimpse of
the gospel and became aware of faith. While remembering
that this is an awesome challenge, are you 'a fragrance' of
Jesus which others will notice? Will they, having met you,
be more open or curious about him?

# Notes

1   Donald B Kraybill, *The Upside Down Kingdom*, Marshall,
Morgan and Scott, 1985, p249.

2   Jim Punton, *The Messiah People*, Hot Iron Press, 1993,
pp8–9.

3   Ronald Sider, *Evangelism and Social Action*, Hodder and
Stoughton, 1993, p74.

**4**    Garth Hewitt, *Walking With Jesus Changes the World*,
Walking With Jesus (audiotape series), Scripture Union,
1990.

*Chapter 8*

# COURAGE

*Jesus identified with the unimportant, the
weak and the sinful, the poor and powerless.
And because he identified with them, to his
critics he became one.*

(Rebecca Pippert)[1]

It was a typical high-spirited Thursday night club, with a dozen
fourteen- and fifteen-year-olds buzzing between the pool table,
the tuck shop and the sponge football that was flying around.
From somewhere, music boomed out at a significant but manage-
able volume. However, the church basement was becoming
stuffy. As windows were opened to let in much needed air, the
level of noise audible outside perceptibly increased. For the man
who lived next door, who had complained before, enough was
enough. He strode purposefully into the building and right into
the centre of the club, where his simmering resentment quickly
spilled over into anger.

The youth club leader, Mac, moved forward, hoping to usher
the complainant into a side-room as he was issuing threats and
telling everyone that the club's days were numbered. Some of the
lads, who were feeling increasingly aggrieved about this uninvited guest, offered to 'deal with' the situation. It is to Mac's credit
that they respected his hasty but polite refusal of their request.
The man left, threatening to report the intolerable noise to the
church authorities.

The lesson I want to draw from this incident does not concern
how to avoid annoying the church's neighbours. Instead, I want
you to appreciate that, as a natural consequence of a successful
piece of youth work, Mac found himself caught in some uncomfortable crossfire.

- The neighbour was annoyed at the volume of music.

- The young people did not appreciate a stranger coming into their club and issuing threats.

- The PCC was upset at the poor relationship generated with the neighbour.

- The caretaker was angry about the fifty pounds' worth of damage done to a curtain in the club room.

- Some of the congregation, who had sensed the tensions surrounding the club, were questioning the value of work with such a rowdy group.

From this one piece of frontier youth work, Mac had become the focus of five different grievances. Being the link, the connection between groups, is sometimes an uncomfortable position to occupy. Reflecting back, I can easily recall how, as Bridges workers, we also experienced the reality of this discomfort.

## Accepting challenging behaviour

As a project, Bridges aimed to build relationships of trust wherever possible. In so doing, especially with hostel residents who arrived after a succession of other options, workers were knowingly taking on a challenge. After a brief honeymoon period, most of these young people would begin to test out the project, seeking to exploit the vulnerability of individual workers and pushing the boundaries of acceptable behaviour. Once this phase had passed, Bridges' consistent care reinforced the message, 'Yes, we want you to stay, we want you to be here, we accept you'. But for the mobile project users, who had previously survived by not putting down roots or allowing themselves to feel too safe, staying at Bridges represented a new and unfamiliar experience. One response was for them to kick harder and be more difficult, asking the question, 'Do you really want me to stay, or will events take a predictable turn and result in a premature end to my stay?' If we seek to provide a key point of renewed hope or trust to those who are scarred or damaged, there will inevitably be challenges along the way.

## Being a safe person

For a significant period of time, Gerry was unemployed and receiving welfare benefits. Whenever his circumstances changed, such as a move to new lodgings, he had to complete a new form and the routine of benefit payments was disrupted. This scenario held many potential frustrations for Gerry: bureaucratic letters could be difficult to understand; or there were delays in payment because information was missing from a new form, or changes to his benefit level because of the different costs of his new accommodation. He often came into Bridges angry, frustrated or unclear about something and wanting to ring the benefits office. Whenever possible, I or another worker would chat to Gerry before he rang and then hover close by in case the call became difficult. This could happen all too easily if Gerry or the benefits advisor approached the conversation with the wrong attitude. It sometimes became necessary for me to speak to the person responsible, and I would listen patiently while this person explained that Gerry's swearing and insults about his or her intelligence could not be tolerated. I would also need to listen as Gerry vented his frustration about his financial struggles or the inadequacies of the benefits advisor. Sometimes it was very difficult to help Gerry get beyond his feelings in order to appreciate any perspective other than his own. Being a safe person will inevitably mean receiving the brunt of aggrieved feelings which have been deflected from their actual target to you.

Going back to the Thursday night club mentioned earlier – Mac was left feeling isolated, undervalued and misunderstood: isolated, because he became the focus for the grievances of five groups of people; undervalued because the neighbour's complaints focused the church's attention exclusively upon the negative aspects of the youth club; and misunderstood, because the caretaker and some others in the church seemed most concerned about fifty pounds' worth of damage to a curtain. Mac is an example of those who give their time to young people, many of whom are disadvantaged, where this contact is the only connection with Jesus they have. Workers like Mac are often on the edge of the church's mission –

visionaries pioneering work in new places or in different ways. It takes boldness and courage to work in this way, but it can be a lonely place.

> There will be anxiety for the worker who moves into this no-man's land between church and community. He (or she) is the living link between different values, attitudes and ideas and will experience the full tension that exists between them. To say that Christian mission must involve this wilderness experience does not eliminate the pain of it.
>
> *(George Lovell)*[2]

It was in response to the challenging aspects of this type of youth work that Frontier Youth Trust first came into being in 1964 , offering a network of support, advice, training and theological reflection to youth workers. When Mac came to see me in my capacity as FYT's field officer in the Eastern counties, the Thursday club was the focus of our long conversation. He needed space and time to share its joys and sorrows with someone who would understand. I think of Mac whenever I read the story of Jesus' arrest. (It is described in Luke 22:39–53 and, in more detail, in Matthew 26:36–56 and Mark 14:32–50). Jesus must have been feeling very isolated at this time: one of his closest friends had betrayed him and the others had run away. No one could possibly understand the agony he was about to face, both physically and spiritually, and the severance of the intimate link he had with his Father. In this most painful moment, Jesus found himself misunderstood, betrayed and abandoned. But he was moving towards the climax of his mission, a climax when all the wrongdoing in the world was brought to the cross. Through him, all people, however ordinary, would potentially be able to make the ultimate connection to God the Father. Jesus made the ultimate sacrifice to secure the greatest prize anyone could ever have.

Jesus' arrest came about because his ministry had brought him into conflict with those who possessed power, authority and status. I will use the story of the man with a paralysed hand, in Luke

6:6–11, to show how this conflict occurred. (You may wish to read the passage at this point.)

## Clash of priorities

While teaching at the synagogue, Jesus noticed the presence of a man with a paralysed hand. Jesus was completely aware of the members of the religious élite who were standing by, and how they would react. What mattered more to him, however, was the restoration of the crippled man to full health. His refusal to defer to the religious, political and social leaders of the day, and his prioritising of the disadvantaged, lost him the respect of many of those with power. In making connections in a similar way, we will also engage in a mission that runs counter to prevailing social values.

> Jesus indicates that if we follow in his way it will probably look like we have 'lost' our life in this world. In other words we may appear like a social failure if we engage in a significant basin ministry.
>
> *(Donald Kraybill)*[3]

## Challenging the status quo

The teachers of the law and the Pharisees were furious that Jesus had healed the man on the Sabbath. His response? 'I ask you: what does our Law allow us to do on the Sabbath? To help or harm?' (Luke 6:9).

The way Jesus lived out God's kingdom values of love and acceptance, particularly among those at the edge, was radically different and a direct challenge to the way the leaders of the day exercised their power. The common people loved Jesus, but the authorities saw him as a threat who needed to be stopped. In making connections with ordinary people, making the marginalised a priority as Jesus did, we will discover the truth of Michael Eastman's words, 'Identification with the powerless inevitably leads to conflict with the powerful.'[4]

## Spiritual authority

Jesus knew that the Pharisees and teachers of the law were closely observing his actions and looking for reasons to accuse him of serious wrongdoing. However, instead of shrinking back, Jesus met them head-on, asking the paralysed man to come to the front of the synagogue. Through his actions Jesus was claiming to possess spiritual authority, and this posed a huge challenge to the chief priests, teachers of the law and the Pharisees who thought they were the key holders to religious insight and virtue.

> The religious establishment moved to destroy Jesus for two reasons: because of his radical socio-economic challenge to the status quo and because of his alleged blasphemy ... they would have to accept Jesus as God's Messiah and only Son. They preferred to kill him.
>
> *(Ron Sider)*[5]

I would like now to tell you how Bridges met its premature end, because in sharing this painful experience, we will touch further upon themes relevant to this chapter.

Julie, co-ordinator at Bridges for most of the project's life, left in June. Nevertheless, our experienced team of four full-time workers, one agency worker and volunteers pressed on with the work. At the end of July, interviews were held by the project's two major funders (the county council and a large national charity), and a new project co-ordinator was appointed. None of the current team, including the deputy, applied for the post, but when the choice was made known, the team felt unhappy about the suitability of the person selected. Significantly, the appointee had not visited the project when it was open, so we did not know what her reaction would be to the busy mêlée of project users (an important litmus test for any new worker). The team held an emergency meeting, and Hannah (the deputy) and I agreed to make our feelings officially known. In response to our phone call the next day, a senior manager from the charity let slip that the appointment had been made for the 'project of the future'. Alarm bells began to ring more loudly.

In August, Bridges had its usual break, but before the traditional September re-opening date arrived official letters were sent to all project users informing them that Bridges would remain closed while a review was taking place. By now the team knew that Bridges' future was at stake, so an off-site campaign headquarters was set up. From there, the team sent out another letter spelling out the urgency of what was happening and urging all users and friends of the project to write to both managing bodies, the county chief of social services or the local Member of Parliament. When people began to visit the project to find out more about the situation, and letters began to arrive on desks, our campaign became widely known. As a consequence, each team member received a verbal warning followed by letters threatening disciplinary action if anything else like this occurred.

Every worker believed that the project users had a right to know what could happen to their project, even though neither they nor the working team were being asked to contribute to the review process. It was all taking place behind closed doors. I have minutes of the meetings we held, the reports we wrote to support our case and the relevant press cuttings. I also have copies of letters that were written in the hope of saving Bridges. Here is an extract from one of them.

A 19-year-old boy, estranged from his family, homeless and involved with drugs. He came into a day-care centre on a Thursday to sit with people like himself. As time went by, he became less and less coherent. Two workers, Julie and Lisa, on duty at the time, noticed this and suspected an overdose. Having observed the boy over the previous three days, they knew he was depressed and guessed what he had done. They got him to hospital and then took care of him when the ordeal was over. As a result of Bridges' actions, no permanent damage was done and the boy is now a healthy 29-year-old.

That man was myself. I went to Bridges because it was the only place I felt I could be with people like myself, a place with understanding and not condemnation. I admit that at 19, and immature, it was a cry for help, but even so Bridges was there for me. They helped me in so many ways ... accommodation, furniture, financial assistance, provided a meal ... If I was stony broke, the others in Bridges would club together and pay for me. I must admit, I feel a little embarrassed, even awkward, in writing this, but I am living proof of the work Bridges has done.

I have sat looking at the joy on children's faces upon their first visit to the fair. I have sat and looked after a roomful of children while the mothers went out shopping or to Stevenage Bowling Alley as a Bridges organised trip. I needn't tell you of the safety value and relief, the importance to some single parents. All provided by fund raising events by Bridges. I have seen so much come from such small beginnings, lives saved, overdoses, even to cut wrists. Men and women who were broken people have become part of the family that Bridges I know is. I've seen them leave Bridges and come back a year later, social circles started at Bridges continuing even now.

Although I am considered to be a man of little integrity and no honour, in prison for nearly four years, I say to you that the very fact that a person like me is taking time out to write this should only go to show the importance of all aspects of the Bridges project...

I ask you to please, please use all your influence and persuasive powers in whatever ways you can to ensure the continuity of Bridges day-centre and the whole Bridges unit. By doing all you can, you will hopefully be ensuring that when another man walks up to the Bridges door, on his last legs having overdosed, he will not find the door closed.

HM Prison, Lewes, East Sussex.

In September and October the strain on us all was considerable. Some days I had a headache, on others I felt ready to explode with anger. During this period Matt, Michael our agency worker and the two new full-time volunteers were asked to leave.

In October, the four senior workers, with nearly twenty years of project experience between us, met with the two managers central to the review. With hindsight, we should have realised that our expectations were unrealistic, but the same strength, hope and resilience that had helped us to work with marginalised young people kept us believing that, through discussion, change was still possible. In reality, the meeting had been planned as the occasion to inform us of decisions that had already been made. At the end of the meeting we were told that the new project would have a different name. As three of us took a sharp intake of breath, Hannah left the room in floods of tears. The new but very limited hostel that was soon to be launched would be a pale reflection of the Bridges Project which had now officially ended.

Quite naturally, it was impossible for many project users, for whom Bridges had been like an extended family, to suddenly end their contact. Although there was no organised activity in the drop-in centre, ongoing support was offered to those who visited. In September alone, we dealt with the eviction of a young family, found an old suicide note at the lodgings of a homeless man, located new accommodation for an eighteen-year-old girl, and talked in depth with an ex-resident who had become pregnant and whose boyfriend and family had conflicting views on what should be done. She travelled ten miles to seek our advice.

On reflection, I believe that Bridges was partly a victim of its style. It was a unique and independent project with an articulate, highly skilled and dedicated co-ordinator in Julie who drew together an excellent and committed team. At all times we were urged to remember that the needs of the project and its users came first, and that management was simply the means by which the work could be supported, resourced and enabled to function more effectively. It never consciously tried to fit into set management structures. It was a project with a mind of its own. Other people (visitors and professionals) rarely had a neutral reaction to the project. Many deeply respected it and felt that it operated in a remarkable way; others had questions about the style and, for some reason, felt uncomfortable with it.

Earlier we looked at the consequences of Jesus' dedication to his mission of making connections with people at the edge. This, I feel, has resonance with our Bridges experience. We rarely sought publicity or wrote articles about ourselves as a model of good working practice. Yet after many years of experience, I now know that its work was highly creative, innovative and mostly excellent. I have a Bridges birthday book here on the desk in front of me, containing the names of 442 different people to whom we sent cards. I myself met hundreds of homeless young people as I ran the lodgings scheme and led sessions on homelessness at local secondary schools.

Bridges was successful, but we did not always play by the rules set down by those who had power in terms of authority and finance. In the end, no one in these positions was prepared to build on the remarkable success of the project by strengthening its weaknesses to move it forward. Instead, they made a strike at our independence and, in doing so, ended a centre that had approximately 150 different contacts each week. There were no plans to replace most of the services Bridges had provided.

A couple of months after Bridges closed, Teresa and her husband, Brian, who were two of our most loyal project users, came to see the new team leader and her line manager. Two weeks later, the same couple came back. After the meeting had ended, the team leader expressed her annoyance that they had had to sit through a second meeting. Teresa and Brian first met at Bridges as homeless teenagers; they had shared each Christmas with Bridges since then; they had celebrated the birth of their children; they had lived through court appearances, prison sentences, relationship break-ups and make-ups – all with Bridges' support. What a tribute that they were now fighting for their project, and how revealing that these two managers could not grasp what Bridges meant to this family!

Much of Bridges' problem was that the decision makers never seemed to fully understand the project. Perhaps they never got close enough to appreciate what really went on.

By now you will have appreciated that I have strong personal feelings about the closure of Bridges. However, the legacy of

Bridges lives on in countless ways. Before concluding this chapter, let us return to the scene of Jesus' arrest (Luke 22:39–53) and reflect on how we, like him, can find the strength to fulfil our mission to make connections, even when it is profoundly uncomfortable, painful and costly.

Jesus' response, in the midst of all the confusion, is incredible. Facing betrayal, aggression, abandonment, misunderstanding and the prospect of a cruel death and agonising separation from his Father, he was able to keep a cool head and remain in control:

- He invited Judas to reflect upon his actions.

- He quelled the violence.

- He healed the wounds of a slave.

- He confronted those arresting him with the inappropriateness of what they were doing.

- He proclaimed the wider spiritual reality of what was taking place.

His example shows us how we too can find invisible resources in the heart of a crisis, in the following ways.

## Drawing on the hidden reserves of prayer

"Then he went off from them about the distance of a stone's throw and knelt down and prayed' (v 41). Jesus' natural reaction to what lay ahead was to turn to his Father. He looked to God to provide the extra strength he needed and would always depend upon. In doing this, 'In great anguish, he prayed even more fervently' (v 44). As his awareness of his need grew stronger, so did the intensity of his prayers.

## Taking a wider view

'But this is your hour, to act when the power of darkness rules' (v 53). His prayerful reliance on his Father gave Jesus the capacity to appreciate the wider implications of the situation in which he found himself. He knew he was about to be arrested, tried and put to death, but had an assurance that in the longer term God knew what he was doing.

When making connections is tough, those who rely upon and are faithful to God will receive, I believe, a reminder that this is a consequence of following him and not a sign of failure. They will also gain an assurance that this is a necessary part of valuable work which God will develop and bless. This affirmation is especially important when others are questioning the value of what you are doing.

## Having clarity of purpose

'Not my will, however, but your will be done' (v 42). Jesus emerged from his anguished prayer before God clearly focused on what he had to do. I believe it is this clarity that enabled him to conduct himself with such remarkable composure in the face of his arrest and betrayal. Jesus worked through his struggles in prayer, and his capacity to confront the situation lovingly was, as a result, greatly increased. Involving God is the key; turning to him, talking with him, grappling with and listening to him gives us strength, assurance of his purposes and coolness to act wisely in difficult times.

In the November of the year Bridges closed, I came back from a Sunday morning church service and felt a need to pray. My thoughts turned to some well known Bible verses and I began to read them. That morning, those familiar words became a living reality for me. For three-quarters of an hour, I savoured each phrase like a box of luxurious Belgian chocolates. Words about God's care, his assurance for my future and his desire that I seek the way ahead, sunk into the depths of my being and left a deep reservoir of peace. It did not remove any frustration, pain or anger, but I knew that God was firmly watching over my journey. I held on to that assurance for the eight months until I was appointed to Frontier Youth Trust. When the going gets tough, the connectors need to turn up their connection to God to keep going!

# Think about

- Read Philippians 2:7–8; Isaiah 40:25–31. (You might like to use the Bible passages as a starting point for prayer or to reflect on the following.)

- Jesus' mission was characterised by commitment, courage and willingness to challenge the status quo, as well as by God's love and compassion. He was obedient unto death.

- Wherever you are, how committed are you to building relationships at the edge? Standing alongside the rejected is painful, listening to the damaged person can be costly, and fighting the cause of the forgotten can feel powerless. In this type of work, it is easy to become a target or to be overlooked, so it requires guts and determination. If you are not directly involved yourself, would you be a close personal support to someone who is?

- Having an overall vision is essential, even if the nuts and bolts are less clear. Being realistic about what you can achieve individually or as a project is also wise.

- Remember that Jesus promised never to leave or forsake us. Ask the Holy Spirit to be your friend and guide. He will sometimes meet you in a special way when you most need him.

# Notes

1   Pippert, *Saltshaker*.

2   George Lovell, *The Church and Community Development*, Avec, 1992, p59.

3   Kraybill, *Upside Down Kingdom*, p298.

4   Michael Eastman was secretary and development officer for Frontier Youth Trust from 1964–1998.

5   Sider, *Evangelism*, pp70–71.

## Chapter 9

# GIVING AND RECEIVING

*She liked all his friends, but most of them
seemed to enjoy her cooking without being
unduly interested in what, if anything, she had
to say. And they did tend to make her feel old
and a little spinsterish ... The feeling with this
man that she didn't have to do anything, or
prove anything, or be responsible for him felt
like a great weight lifting off her shoulders...*

(Kathy Galloway)[1]

Here are two questions to introduce the themes we will be looking at in this chapter. The first is, should passers-by give money
to the beggars who sit on the pavements and subways of our
major conurbations? And the second, in the story of Jesus' visit to
the home of Martha, Mary and Lazarus (Luke 10:38-42), with
which character do you most identify?

What these two questions have in common (other than that
they often generate much discussion) is that they touch on a similar theme, namely, that of polarisation – people who are working
and those who are not; the deserving and the undeserving; people
who serve and those who are being served – issues that quickly
strike a human chord and that are related to the crucial issue of
grace, which was at the heart of Jesus' mission.

The passage in Luke noted above (you may wish to read it at
this point, or turn to it for reference) has prompted me, as always,
to reflect on my encounters with people at Bridges; but, more
unusually, it has also triggered wider questions about how we
worked with people at the centre. Furthermore, the story offers
insights into the kind of relationship Jesus wants to have with his

disciples, and how this shapes the way we make connections with others in his name. In this chapter, there are three issues to grapple with, which come under the general theme of giving and receiving.

## Giving and being with

The Gospels reveal to us that Jesus' visit to Martha, Mary and Lazarus was not the only one he had made. In the early part of John chapter 11, Jesus had gone to Bethany even though people there had wanted to stone him. The passage gives a reason for his resolve: 'Jesus loved Martha and her sister and Lazarus' (v 5). This was a family who warmly welcomed Jesus and whom he had come to know well – sufficiently intimately, in fact, to enable both sisters to have considerable confidence in his power to bring their brother back to life, and for Martha to proclaim, 'I do believe that you are the Messiah, the Son of God, who was to come into the world' (v 27).

On the occasion of Jesus' visit described in Luke chapter 10, Martha was preparing a meal. This meant that her time and energy were taken up elsewhere and she was unable to be part of the main company, talking with Jesus and listening to his teaching. There are always jobs to be done if a family, community or organisation is to function effectively. On the days that visitors to Bridges could stay into the early evening, one person was usually asked to take overall charge of food preparation. However, workers were encouraged to ask project users to help. Meal preparation, crèche duty and taking visitors home in the mini-bus, all presented opportunities for them to take part and for a significant conversation to take place.

To be honest, there were frequent occasions when it seemed far easier to do it all yourself, and I am sure that many team members, like me, sometimes did so. And there were times when a worker was feeling sensitive or bruised from an encounter and needed to be alone with their thoughts. In my case, as my role became more community-focused, there were a lot of projects or follow-up work which took me away from the hubbub of the centre. But this move to the periphery, though necessary, was also accompanied by the temptation to keep at a distance from the nitty-gritty of the insults, tensions, comical banter and exchanges at the centre's focus. Throughout my working life, placing myself in the thick of it remained the greatest challenge. It was never simple! However, skirting round the edges never felt satisfactory either, and whenever I succumbed to the temptation I denied myself the richness and variety of life at Bridges. My experience of our last ever Christmas dinner was a timely reminder of this.

Our Yuletide meal raised a number of problems. How would we fit around thirty adults into the Bridges living-room? Who would keep all the children upstairs fed, watered and occupied? And finally, when would the food fight start and how long would it last? Having worked hard to prepare food, it is discouraging to see roasted projectiles hurtling across the room. Fellow-worker Matt and I came up with the idea of some post-meal entertainment (other than the flying food, that is!). We felt it important to give this good publicity, so we made sure that conversations on the day included mention of a surprise and, to arouse curiosity, I taped an 'order of events' to each table. This ensured that people knew the predictable routine would be broken and made it less likely that the food fight was the final event of the day.

On the day itself, I found myself feeling reasonably at ease and confident about our plans, and decided to sit in the middle seat of one of the tables rather than stay aloof and serve food. It turned out to be much greater fun than I imagined. I really enjoyed laughing along with the project users, and made the best of the occasion and their company. I was also in a better position to quell the early food skirmish. When the inevitable conflict broke out, all remaining plates were quickly removed, tables cleared and people's attention diverted, because everyone knew that there was more action to follow. By the time Matt and I had started our impression of 'Staying Alive' by the Bee Gees, complete with glitter wigs and painfully high voices, I already knew that the show would be a great success, even though it was destined to remain a one-hit wonder!

Back to Luke chapter 10 – Martha had become upset. I wonder which bothered her more? Was is the fact that having to prepare the food denied her the chance to be with the others? Or was it because Mary was (as usual) not doing her share of the work? Jesus' words – 'Martha, Martha! You are worried and troubled over so many things' (v 41) – gives no specific interpretation of her feelings. However, Kathy Galloway's imaginative description of the scene includes speculation on the nature of Martha's frustration:

> Just for once, she'd have liked to put down the burden of responsibility for the endless loads of people to feed ... and put in her little bit. She had thoughts, didn't she, about life and the world ... she was fed up with being the one who made it happen for everyone else ... she felt shut out, hurt, pushed to the edge.[2]

Whether this interpretation is accurate or not, Jesus stated clearly to Martha that her worries and troubles were an unnecessary distraction. I am certain that he wanted very much to spend time with her, to share his fellowship with the whole person he loved. While not wishing to devalue her hard work, we can see how Martha's preoccupation kept her on the edge and limited her capacity for a meaningful encounter with anyone, let alone Jesus. The same is true for us. Keeping at a safe distance and having an over-emphasis on getting practical details just right will hinder our mission to make meaningful connections with other people.

## Being open to receiving, dignity and value

> As Jesus and his disciples went on their way, he came to a village where a woman named Martha welcomed him into her home.
>
> *(Luke 10:38)*

Martha felt a special responsibility because this was her home and being a good hostess meant a lot to her. She was used to serving others (see John 12:2). It was in her nature to want to give, to show how much she valued and appreciated her guests by providing the best possible meal for them. These are honourable intentions. But when Martha's feelings came to a head and she appealed to Jesus for support, he refused to affirm that her priorities were the right ones. Maybe in being so intent on giving she was missing out.

Determination was a hallmark of my first weeks at the Bridges project – determination to embrace this new challenge, to learn from the experience, to make the project a genuine base for living and not to escape to family and friends too often, and to be committed to serving the project users as best I could. After only a few days, however, Julie, tempered my surge of enthusiasm by reminding me that I needed my personal space. After a full day's work in the drop-in centre, I would often spend the evenings playing cards with hostel residents. I was wearing myself out! One day, some months later, I was sitting in the Bridges' office, feeling weary and a bit low, and fully-appreciating that a person can only give so much. It had been a long and busy day, and my mood was not helped by something I had said earlier to fellow-worker Lorna, which had come out all wrong and which she had resented. As a subdued Lorna was clearing up close by, Dane walked in looking for a light. I had a box of matches for just such occasions, and passed them to him.

'He's a good chap,' Dane said to Lorna.

Although this may have fallen on unimpressed ears, I was already feeling encouraged before he continued, 'I like you, Tim. A lot of people think a lot of you around here, you know.'

I was far too taken aback to come out with a suitably grateful response. But, as I let Dane's healing words of affirmation seep into my consciousness, my mood was transformed and my energy renewed. The ride home in the car with Lorna not only passed pleasantly but gave me a chance to be reconciled with her.

This is the first example I recall of something we instinctively knew about life at Bridges: that we would receive from the project users as well as giving to them. It is foolish to rely on consistent words of comfort or praise from others, but it is also unwise to be so focused on our giving that we fail to notice or appreciate the positive contribution of those whom we seek to serve.

A voluntary poverty of mind makes professionals open to receive constantly new knowledge and insight from those who help. When we can work for the poor in the spirit of receptivity and gratitude our help can be accepted without shame.

*(Henri Nouwen)*[3]

The danger of being entirely focused on giving was highlighted powerfully for me a few months after Bridges had ended. I knew Gerald quite well because I had found him lodgings a couple of times and, like Callum, he had occasionally visited me at home. One mid December, Gerald came to the flat. His accommodation arrangements had broken down and he was about to be homeless. After vainly trying to help him find local lodgings, I agreed to let him use the flat for two or three weeks over the Christmas period. This meant us sharing for the first week, then I left Gerald to stay while I went to my parents over Christmas (he joined us on Boxing Day). The Sunday before Christmas, I invited Gerald along to a large youth fellowship I was attending, and he settled in well. Afterwards, I came away with numerous cards and a handful of presents. I felt awkward because Gerald had been given just one card. He seemed quiet and ill at ease on the journey home in the car.

Sometime the next day, Gerald returned home from a trip out and produced a brown paper bag: 'I felt so awkward with everyone giving you things, I've got you these. Not much, I know, but thanks.' The gloves were a kind enough gift, but the gesture itself was far more significant. I had been so sure that his quietness the previous day had been the result of not receiving any gifts, when he had actually been thinking how he could find a way to give. I had underestimated him. Serving selflessly is honourable; however, unless we are watchful, it is easy to slip into a cosy self-satisfaction. With Gerald, the uncomfortable truth was that I was accustomed to thinking of him as someone who needed charity, and not as a person wishing to give or who had a positive contribution to make.

Bob Lupton, of FCS's Urban Ministries in Atlanta, also discovered the importance of retaining the dignity of those we serve.

At Christmas they were used to running a scheme in which their more affluent contacts presented gifts to needy families in the inner city. However, Bob and the others began to notice how embarrassed some families were to receive in this way, so a significant adjustment took place in their methods. Gifts were donated as before, but were left unwrapped and made up the stock for a Christmas toy shop at the centre. Goods were labelled at a price accessible to all; but for those with no resources, jobs were created around the new shop or the centre itself, so that everyone could buy presents. Bob Lupton reflects:

> Our past one-way giving had subtly communicated 'you have nothing of worth which we desire in return.' We determined then and there that all of our future giving would enhance human dignity and strengthen the hands of parents as providers.[4]

## Journeying with others

Martha liked to be the hostess, the person with the responsibility for ensuring that her guests were well looked after. Jesus was a friend she loved and respected, so naturally she tried to provide the best she could. But when she looked to Jesus for help, all he said was 'Mary has chosen the right thing, and it will not be taken away from her' (Luke 10:42). Mary – who, as far as Martha was concerned, was partly responsible for her problems – was being held up as a model from which Martha could learn. It didn't seem fair.

If we step back for a moment and consider the implication of Jesus' reply, we will appreciate the radical nature of his invitation. Martha not only knew her duties as a hostess but also her accustomed place as a woman – in the kitchen serving the needs of the men in her home. Furthermore, in the religious culture of those times, women were excluded from learning the law (Torah) and had to rely on the beneficence of men (to whom they were related as sisters, daughters and wives) to pass that knowledge on to them. In other words, women held no spiritual identity of their own. This may be why Martha may have been expecting Jesus gently to usher Mary into the kitchen. Instead, by implication, he invited Martha to join them. She too had permission to break convention, to come and reflect, discuss, listen and learn as a person in her own right!

Jesus' challenge to Martha echoes his words in John's Gospel, spoken to his disciples: 'I do not call you servants any longer, because servants do not know what their master is doing. Instead, I call you friends, because I have told you everything I have heard from my Father' (John 15:15). This is the greatest invitation we can ever receive, but it also throws up many challenges. There are many times when my selfish wishes take me away, consciously or unconsciously, from Jesus. There are moments when I want to echo Simon Peter's words in Luke 5:8: 'Go away from me, Lord! I am a sinful man!' Jesus' desire for friendship can make us feel uncomfortable, as it did Martha.

Meanwhile, Mary seems more serene. The image of her sitting intently at the feet of the Lord is an evocative one. It reminds me of the wide-eyed child curled up at the feet of a parent or grandparent, eagerly awaiting words that will interest and amuse, captivate and enthuse, teach and inspire. Mary appears to want to hear all Jesus has to say. She has discovered the ultimate storyteller who will tell her about life in general and her own life in particular. She wants to remain close to him in case some of his holiness rubs off. She stays by his side because there she feels secure and special. Jesus desires that we travel with him as his disciples and his companions, staying close enough to him and to each other to learn together. Mary was in the best position for this to happen.

Bridges was most successful in helping homeless young people and disadvantaged young families to belong. Scores of vulnerable, rootless people arrived and found not only shelter but a home and a community. Many went on to form their own families and were housed locally. The project was skilful at adapting to changing needs so that people could stay in touch until their mid-twenties or beyond. And project users were encouraged to be mutually supportive. What was never achieved at Bridges, though, was the transition of very experienced project users into helpers. This would have been a difficult task, but I regretted afterwards that people we had known for over five years could not have at least been challenged to become more involved by taking on some responsibility. Perhaps we should have consciously sought to develop their knowledge of how Bridges worked, and given them a sense of stake-holding and empowerment.

Let us go back to Luke chapter 5, when Jesus called the first disciples. The incident ends with Jesus concluding, 'Don't be afraid; from now on you will be catching people'; so 'they pulled the boats up on the beach, left everything, and followed Jesus' (vs 10–11). This is a remarkable change of lifestyle that these fisherman are making! They had little idea of what lay ahead. They knew what they were leaving, but not what they were taking on. They probably had aspirations, but no clue as to the reality of what would follow. They admired Jesus and wondered about him, but did they really know for sure who he was? This was the start of a journey in which most of their discoveries would be made along the way and not before they started. As they travelled together, as well as getting to know Jesus as a companion, they were becoming his disciples. They were being taught and trained; and, crucially, Jesus was revealing to them his identity and his mission – a mission they would later adopt: 'All this is done by God, who through Christ changed us from enemies into his friends and gave us the task of making others his friends also' (2 Cor 5:18).

There were many times at Bridges when I talked to people about my belief in Jesus, or about faith in general. (I am also only too aware of the numerous occasions when my weariness or wish to avoid potential conflict allowed possible openings to pass.) However, I could always foresee how awkward it might be if one of the project users began to show a greater interest in Jesus. I can now appreciate why I felt that way. If Dane, for example, had become a Christian, he would have become a 'brother', a friend, companion and fellow disciple. I would have had to take on a significant role in supporting and encouraging him in his new faith. For me, this would have caused a confusion of roles. While I cared very much for Dane and the others I served at Bridges, none of them became my friends in a fuller sense. The prospect of relating to Dane as a project user *and* as a fellow-Christian and friend seemed awkward. Perhaps I would be accused of favouritism. This is the kind of dilemma faced by many Christians working in similar situations.

It seems to me that building relationships, or friendships, at the edge, making disciples and evangelising are much more integrated than we might expect, though this in no way detracts from the significance and distinctiveness of these three strands of the Christian faith.

> The way of Jesus and the prophets isn't just a welfare programme; it calls for a change of heart, a revolution of the spirit, a transformation of our consciousness, it moves us beyond the familiar options of abandoning the poor, controlling the poor, or even helping the poor from places of isolation and comfort. Instead, it leads us to a new relationship with one another, a deep connection.
>
> *(Jim Wallis)*[5]

## Think about

- Read Luke 5:1–11; 2 Corinthians 5:16–19. (You might like to use the Bible passages as a starting point for prayer or to reflect on the following.)

- When considering Luke 10:38–42, are you more like Martha or Mary? Do you find it easier to give or to receive?

- Are you more comfortable with practical tasks rather than mixing with people? Does this keep you at a distance and hinder you in terms of building relationships with others?

- If you are working with those at the edge, or planning to, will your way of working ensure that the self-esteem and dignity of those to whom you are committed are retained and enhanced? Is there flexibility to enable them to take on some responsibility?

- If anyone begins to show interest in becoming more involved, taking time to describe the project's Christian ethos to them is an opportunity to tell a story of faith, and to encourage them to reflect on what commitment to the project means. Many need to belong before they believe; being a co-worker or volunteer may help this to happen.

## Notes

1   Galloway, *Imagining the Gospels*, p68.

2   Galloway, p67.

3   Nouwen, *Reaching Out*, p98.

4   Bob Lupton, *Urban Perspectives*, FCS Ministries.

5   Wallis, *Politics*, p164.

## Chapter 10

# GOD WITH US

*The people of Jesus' day thought holy men
were unapproachable. But Jesus' work was in
the marketplace. He made people feel
welcome, and that they had a place. His life
was a constant demonstration that there were
only two things that mattered in this life – God
and people. They were the only things that
lasted for ever.*

(Rebecca Pippert)[1]

If I was permitted only one word to sum up all that has been
written so far, it would be 'with'. Indeed, the chapter headings
I have chosen deliberately emphasise various aspects of this
connectedness.

**Arrival** – being physically *with* those at Bridges.

**Contact** – being *with* them in the sense of getting alongside.

**Discovery** – being close enough to see their pain, personality
and potential, to understand the human emotions I shared
*with* them.

**Space** – being *with* in the sense of creating space to listen and
understand.

**Identification** – the consequence of being *with* people long
enough to begin to see the world through their eyes.

**Readiness** – being *with* them enough to know how to use free
spaces and fluid phases wisely.

**Linking** – helping others link together; sometimes being the link that enables them to reach an understanding *with* someone.

**Courage** – being committed to the disadvantaged can be difficult and lonely. People in positions of power and influence will not necessarily give you resources or respect you for your choice. Many will be against rather than *with* you.

**Giving and receiving** – being willing to give of yourself, and being able to receive and to empower. Finally, being *with* someone ultimately means travelling together and becoming friends.

Throughout this journey, Jesus has been our role model, the person to follow, the example to emulate. His coming to earth made this possible, but he paid the price for his choice; he suffered the ultimate disconnection, the severing of his relationship with the Father:

> When God himself in his humanity became part of our most painful experience of God's absence, he became most present to us ... In Jesus, God became one of us to lead us through Jesus into the intimacy of his divine life.
>
> *(Henri Nouwen)*[2]

On the cross Jesus suffered agony and shame. He died outside the city gates, outside of God's grace, so that ordinary people could be with God in a new and intimate way. The challenge for Christians is to follow Jesus' example and to make connections in his name. Through the Holy Spirit, Jesus lives in us; as we continually make ourselves available to him, we can trust that others will be affected by the presence of the Spirit working in and through us.

I hope that this book has not left you overawed by the challenge of following Jesus, even if you are overwhelmed by the wonder of him. But however you feel, I want to conclude with some reflections drawing on themes we have already touched on, to give us encouragement, direction and hope.

## With humanity

One of my most striking impressions of Jesus is that the people who were considered by society to be the worst sinners, who were assumed by the pious to be excluded from God's plans, were usually most attracted to him – and he welcomed them. Why then, if God's Son related to people in this way, do some Christians still act as though embracing the notion of holiness means staying well clear of others who are different from themselves. Is this based on a feeling of superiority? Insecurity? Some kind of discomfort with their own humanity? I readily admit to feeling all three during my time as a Bridges worker; the project was such a demanding environment, it put me in touch with my human weakness. However, I discovered that, as I became more honest with myself about these parts of my make-up, I found it easier to empathise with and care for the project users. Having a faith in Jesus did not prevent me from finding out how much I had in common with them in our shared vulnerability and humanity in a fallible world.

> Christians from my own tradition have most often sought
> to emphasise their difference and distinctiveness. I wonder
> if the time has not come for us to stress our commonality,
> and let any difference speak for itself. The parable of the
> Pharisee and the Publican ( Luke 18:9–14), tells us that
> the claim 'I am not like other people' is always a
> blasphemy. Our salvation does not remove our humanity,
> but releases it to reach its potential,
>
> *(Mark Riddell)*³

Let us, therefore, ask God not only to forgive our frailties but to give us the commitment, grace and strength to overcome the barriers that prevent us from making connections with those who are different.

> I deceive myself if I feel my spirituality makes it harder to
> communicate with people around me. True spirituality
> makes me more ordinary, more easy to know.
>
> *(John White)*⁴

## With hope

It would be wrong to assume automatically that working with people at the edge is discouraging or depressing. In fact, working at Bridges brought true meaning to the word hope. Somehow, working alongside those who were at the bottom of the pile, or who had suffered greatly in their lives, helped me to appreciate the nature of hope. Their capacity to keep going despite the problems was humbling. It helped me to put life into perspective. I learnt to rejoice in the small signs of progress, to discern the little shoots of hope and to relish the lighter moments when they came. Certainly standing alongside the marginalised, in the knowledge that God was especially committed to their welfare, stirred something deep within me that was poignant, passionate and hopeful. Hope can sustain us, help us to persevere, renew our strength and keep us believing that people will develop in a positive way. We must hold on to our hope in Christ, especially when our project or church mission becomes discouraging or exhausting.

I wonder whether having nowhere left to turn made it easier for people to take a risk and come to Jesus; whether having nothing to lose spurred them on to take a step of faith. Jesus always approached those he met with great hope, with a certainty based on his relationship with his Father, and with a confidence in his own God-given ability and authority. For those of us who sometimes feel less certain, hope in God provides strength when we feel weak and vision when the external signs are less encouraging. It is also a witness to others that we have an unseen source of life, a link to something greater than ourselves.

> The sense of God's grace and the awareness of the activity of the Holy Spirit means that we are not linked to what is feasible in human terms. On occasions, courageous confidence allows us to move beyond issues of viability and aspire to an outcome which is greater than might be anticipated from the objective evidence, for prayerfulness and trust in God do make a difference.
>
> *(Ann Morisy)*[5]

# With humility

Shola and Marjorie were local volunteers and the backbone of the Bridges' main room when I first started at the project. They were remarkable. Marjorie's heart and lungs were weak, and she had a pacemaker installed so that she could function as effectively as possible. She had been involved in Bridges since its earliest days and for many years organised the birthday cards and prison letters sent to project users. She and her husband Toby (the swimmer from chapter one) regularly invited the three full-time volunteers to their home on a Wednesday evening. It was always a warm and welcome break. Marjorie was chirpy, occasionally tetchy, but she had great commitment and compassion. When she died, still awaiting a heart-and-lung transplant, the Catholic church she and Toby attended was packed out with project users, despite the fact that Bridges had been closed for months.

Shola was equally unique. She was a huge woman whose enormity was only matched by her capacity to empathise with those who felt down on themselves. Her self-image was greatly affected by her size, and she suffered from bouts of depression which at one time developed into mental breakdown. However, she managed to channel her energies in two ways. First, she was a conscientious and effective peace campaigner, well-known for her ability to create a roadblock. When Shola sat down in the road to protest, it took five policemen to move her! She also came regularly to Bridges and talked to people in the main room. Many of the most unlikely characters found a friend in Shola, and she could regularly be seen placing a large loving arm around the shoulder of someone who needed reassurance and understanding. About four years before Marjorie's death, Shola's body began to give out and, after a lengthy illness, she died. Most of the project users were bitterly upset to lose her, and I know I shall never meet anyone like her again.

Marjorie and Shola represent my answer to anyone who thinks that the task of making connections with people at society's edge is too daunting and only for the exceptionally gifted or the especially trained. Jesus himself took on the vulnerability of human form before embarking on a mission to save the world, and he chose disciples who were neither learned or the cream of society. In the same way, without seeing how they related to project users, I would not have identified Shola or Marjorie as typical Bridges volunteers. But the obvious solution is not always the most effective; human wisdom and God-given wisdom are not necessarily the same.

Marjorie and Shola had two qualities which were needed at Bridges, which are also, I believe, needed by those who seek to make connections in Jesus' name: they did not think too highly of themselves, and they knew from their own experience what it meant to suffer. The danger of a person having too much self-respect is that as well as failing to see one's own weakness, one can easily lose sympathy with the faults, failings and fallibility of others. The strength of those who suffer is that they have a greater awareness of what it feels like to struggle and to need help. They are therefore sensitive to the words and actions which may bring consolation, and can relate with the compassion that was evident in the lives of Shola and Marjorie.

## Walking with

Another feature of Jesus' ministry in Luke's Gospel came as a surprise. For many years, my overall impression of him had been that he was principally an initiator. In the light of this example, the evangelistic task appeared to follow naturally: 'Go then, to all the peoples everywhere and make them my disciples' (Matt 28:19). But, as I read about 'Mob', the woman who suffered from bleeding, the prostitute who wept at Jesus' feet, blind Bartimaeus and Martha, I realised that the crucial part of those encounters took place when each of them had taken the initiative. Only after Jesus' presence had prompted them to respond to him in some way, did he employ his instinct and insight to perceive and affirm their actions and help them make life-changing connections.

The autobiography of Patricia St John was recently given to me by her sister Hazel.[6] During her lifetime, Patricia felt guided by God to go to Tangier in North Africa. It was fascinating to read her description of the process by which she became established in the community and shared her faith. Initially, she concentrated on studying Arabic and practised the language by talking to a few local women she knew. She describes this as a time of 'learning, growing and discovering'. After a while some local boys came to visit her, out of curiosity and because they were hungry. While feeding them with the little extra she had, she told them the story of the Good Shepherd. Weeks later, one of the boys asked her to visit his family who were eager to ask this foreign lady lots of questions. A significant breakthrough came when the son of a wealthy local family became ill and, as someone known to be a nurse, Patricia was asked to help. Over the following months and years there were further opportunities for her to develop her work in the community and to talk about her faith in Jesus. Patricia's story reinforced my impression of Jesus' approach and of my experiences at Bridges. The key is always to be among people, observing, learning how others tick, responding to their wishes where possible, developing relationships and talking about faith at a pace they are comfortable with. Then, through prayer, faithfulness and the use of God-given abilities, we can make effective connections with those among whom we live and to whom we are committed. I am continually reminded that effective faith-sharing is relational not formal, involves being alongside not above, and is first about listening and then sharing. Furthermore, God does not need us to produce him from somewhere, like a rabbit out of a hat: he is already present and at work; he simply asks us to be available.

When Jesus called his first disciples, he said, 'Follow me', which literally means 'Come to the place where I am standing'. He wanted them to be people who walked with him. He told his disciples that they were no longer servants but friends: servants walked behind their masters, friends walked *with* them. For the disciples, the journey alongside Jesus was a series of struggles and surprises, but also a constant learning process. If, as Christians, we want to make connections so as to help others become disciples, then we will need to invite people to accompany us on the journey as we faithfully follow Jesus. As they walk with us, they will have the opportunity to glimpse how this is also a walk with someone else. Like the two disciples on the road to Emmaus, their hearts may 'burn' as they sense the presence of Jesus.

> Evangelism ... is the invitation to say 'yes' to joining the
> mission of God – to travelling hopefully to new and
> unexplored places in the company of those who want to be
> part of God's coming Kingdom ... Faith is to recognise
> and respond to the presence of that God who invites all
> humanity to relationship with one another, with creation
> and with Father, Son and Spirit.
>
> *(Robin Greenwood)*[7]

Robin Greenwood is writing with the task of the local church as
his focus. Although *Making Connections* principally reflects the
setting at Bridges, I firmly believe that what I have discovered has
significance for mission in other contexts. For Christians genuinely committed to building relationships at the edge, there is
potentially real benefit to be gained from doing this as a church
project. Indeed, I am currently seeking to apply the learning within the community ministry of my own local church.

Bridges possessed many of the elements of a close-knit community: a network of supportive relationships, a sense of
belonging, times of celebration, an opportunity to contribute by
helping the project, and the chance to meet and talk to others on a
similar journey. What is distinctive about a church or mission is
that it is Jesus who draws people together, who has prompted the
work. Alongside the key purpose of building community, building
relationships with people at the edge is intended to enable them to
acknowledge that the key focus is Jesus. Where a church project
can introduce people to their life as a worshipping community,
aspects such as prayer, worship and reflecting on God's word may
also touch their hearts through the Holy Spirit. The coming together of Christians in this way provides an opportunity for those at the
edge to discover the reality of the extra dimension of Jesus' presence: 'Where two or three come together in my name I am there
with them' (Matt 18:20).

There were occasions at Bridges when difficult circumstances
could have deteriorated into very serious ones, but events
predominantly took a positive turn and damage was limited. At

these moments Julie would conclude, 'Well, we do say that God is somehow looking after us.' It was in the most difficult circumstances, when there was a sense of just having to trust, that Julie and others could most easily affirm God's presence.

Amongst my Bridges' experiences, it was the closing down of the project that was the most painful. The predominant focus and motivation for my mission over six and a half years, the environment that I had been such a part of and helped to shape, began to be dismantled. Suddenly, after managing the project, the team lost all influence; the project users were hardly kept informed, let alone consulted; and those in the decision-making positions kept tight hold of the power they had. Yet Jim Wallis believes (as Julie pinpointed) that it is in the experience of powerlessness that a profound truth emerges:

> The slaves knew powerlessness, and out of it they found the power beyond themselves ... It's the complete giving that unlocks power. Never achievement or success – certainly not for Jesus, but rather the giving of ourselves in faith leads to life. In that powerlessness lies the real spiritual power.[8]

I drove past the former site of the Bridges project one day and discovered that the buildings had been almost totally demolished. Only a solitary brick archway was left standing. The sight was so poignant, I stopped the car to reflect.

Now, I want you to imagine that you are standing, facing that archway. You are aware that this is an entrance leading to a position at the edge. You pause to peer through to see what lies beyond. You can see the crumbling structures – these represent the damaged areas of people's lives. Some walls are completely knocked down, like the brokenness within people, and the victims and casualties can be seen in the rubble. But I am urging you still to take a step forward and to walk through, to accept the challenge. If you do, you will be surprised by the variety of precious stones you find hidden in the rubble. There will be rough diamonds – a little sharp and grubby but which can be softened and polished. And there are the older gems, which may take a little time to discover because of the dirt and dust – but you will find them. By committing yourself to being there, you will begin to understand the pain and brokenness in your own life amid the debris, which will become useful tools in your work.

Before you decide whether or not to go to the edge, you must do one final thing. Look again at the archway. Focus in particular on the stone at the pinnacle of the archway. That is called the capstone (or cornerstone) and is the name used to describe Jesus (1 Peter 2:7). Notice how it is strong enough to support the structure and keep it standing: you will need this strength to sustain your mission. See how the capstone provides a connection, is the meeting point of the two bricked sides of the archway. Jesus is the perfect example to emulate in terms of building relationships at the edge. And lastly, remember that without this stone there would be no entrance standing there. Jesus is the means by which we gain access into God's presence.

I earnestly hope and pray that Jesus prompts you to take up the challenge. It will not be comfortable, but it will inspirationally change both yours and other's lives.

## Notes

1   Pippert, *Saltshaker*, p36.

2   Nouwen, *Reaching Out*, p115.

3   Mike Riddell, 'Every disciple is in the same boat', *Third Way*, November 1996.

4   John White, *Changing on the Inside*, Eagle, 1991, p190.

5   Ann Morisy, *Beyond the Good Samaritan: Community ministry and mission*, Mowbray, 1997, p120.

6   Patricia is best known as the writer of the children's Christian novel, *Treasures in the Snow*.

7   Robin Greenwood, *Practising Community*, SPCK, 1996, pp55–56.

8   Wallis, *Politics*, p214.

# BIBLIOGRAPHY

Christine Acheson, 'The Bridge Community Project', *News*, April 1996, Churches Community Work Alliance.

Dave Andrews, *Can You Hear the Heartbeat*, Hodder and Stoughton, 1989; *Building a Better World*, Lion, 1996.

Bailey, Bristow and Dorton, *Worlds Apart*, Frontier Youth Trust (FYT, Yorkshire and Humberside), 1994.

T R and M Batten, *The Non-directive Approach*, Avec, 1988.

F Beckett, *Called to Action*, Fount, HarperCollins, 1989.

Mike Breen, *Outside In*, Scripture Union, 1993.

John Buckeridge, 'People not programmes', *Youthwork*, October–November 1995.

Patrick Butler, 'If black is black', *Mayflower Youth Work*, September 1983.

R J Cassidy and P J Scharper, *Political Issues in Luke–Acts*, Orbis, 1983.

Lawrence J Crabb, *Moving Through Your Problems Toward Finding God*, Scripture Press, 1994.

Lawrence J Crabb and Dan B Allender, *Encouragement: The Key to Caring*, Navpress, 1986.

Juan Damián, 'The Latin American churches and evangelism', *Ecumenical Letter on Evangelism*, August 1996.

Terry Dunnell, *Mission and Young People at Risk*, FYT, 1995; *Keys and Pegs*, Spiritual Development Project, FYT.

Michael Eastman (ed), *Inside Out*, CPAS, 1976.

K Erickson, 'Notes on the sociology of deviance', *The Other Side: Perspectives on Deviance*, H S Becker (ed), Free Press United States.

M Fearon, *With God on the Frontiers*, Scripture Union, 1988; *No Place Like Home*, SPCK, 1989.

Kathy Galloway, *Imagining the Gospels*, SPCK, 1994.

Robin Greenwood, *Practising Community*, SPCK, 1996.

Garth Hewitt, *Walking With Jesus Changes the World*, Walking With Jesus (audiotape series), Scripture Union, 1990.

R T Kendall, *The Holy Spirit and Forgiveness*, Walking With Jesus (audiotape series), Scripture Union, 1992.

Donald B Kraybill, *The Upside Down Kingdom*, Marshall, Morgan and Scott, 1985.

P Logan, *A Life to be Lived*, Darton, Longman and Todd, 1989.

Tim Lovejoy, 'Remains of the day', *News*, Autumn 1996, FYT.

George Lovell, *The Church and Community Development*, Avec, 1992.

Robert Lupton, *Urban Perspectives*, FCS Ministries.

Floyd McClung, *The Father Heart of God*, Kingsway, 1998.

Ann Morisy, *Beyond the Good Samaritan: Community ministry and mission*, Mowbray, 1997.

M Morse, *The Unattached*, Penguin, 1965.

Henri Nouwen, *Reaching Out: The three movements of the spiritual life*, Fount, HarperCollins, 1980.

Leanne Payne, *The Healing Presence: Healing in your broken places, living God's love*, Kingsway, 1990.

Rebecca Pippert, *Out of the Saltshaker: Evangelism as a way of life*, Inter-Varsity Press, 1980.

John Powell, *He Touched Me: My pilgrimage of prayer*, Tabor, 1974; *The Christian Vision*, Argus, 1984.

John Powell and Loretta Brady, *Will the Real Me Please Stand Up*, Argus, 1985.

Jim Punton, *Mission*, FYT, 1971; *The Messiah People*, Hot Iron Press, 1993.

Mike Riddell, 'Every disciple is in the same boat', *Third Way*, November 1996.

Roger Sainsbury, *Middle-classes keep out – Advice to incomers on entering the inner city*, Greenbelt, August 1981.

Joan Searle, *The Importance of Listening*, Guild of Health, 1984.

David Sheppard, *Bias to the Poor*, Hodder and Stoughton, 1984; 'The poverty that imprisons the spirit', *The Listener*, April 1984.

Ronald Sider, *Evangelism and Social Action*, Hodder and Stoughton, 1993.

*Patricia St John Tells Her Own Story*, Operation Mobilisation, 1995.

Elaine Storkey, *The Search for Intimacy*, Hodder and Stoughton, 1995.

J Townsend, *Hiding from Love*, Scripture Press, 1992.

A Twelvetrees, *Community Work*, Macmillan, for British Association of Social Workers, 1982.

Colin Urquhart, *My Dear Son*, Hodder and Stoughton, 1992.

Jean Vanier, *The Challenge of L'Arche*, Darton, Longman and Todd, 1982.

Jim Wallis, *The Soul of Politics*, HarperCollins, 1995.

Robert Warren, *Building Missionary Congregations*, Church House Publishing, 1995.

John White, *Changing on the Inside*, Eagle, 1991; *Eros Redeemed: Breaking the stranglehold of sexual sin*, Eagle, 1993.

P Wilson, *Gutter Feelings*, Marshall, Morgan and Scott, 1985.